FREEING RAPUNZEL

MAKING PEACE FROM HER TRAUMA IN A DIVIDED HOMELAND

ANNE-CHRISTINE WITZGALL

Freeing Rapunzel

Copyright © 2021 by Anne-Christine Witzgall

All rights reserved

Published by Red Penguin Books

Bellerose Village, New York

Library of Congress Control Number: 2022900076

ISBN

Print 978-1-63777-210-2

Digital 978-1-63777-211-9

No part of this book may be reproduced in any form or by any electronic or mechanical means, including information storage and retrieval systems, without written permission from the author, except for the use of brief quotations in a book review.

Für Aaron und Adrian

"Life in itself is an inexplicable miracle; to be alive is a manifestation of that miracle."
Gao Xingjian from "One Man's Bible"

CONTENTS

Prologue	1

PART 1
1. Men In My Room	11
2. Like Rapunzel In The Tower	17
3. Betrayal	21
4. Hands Tell The Truth	27
5. Nurse	31
6. When You Get Married, Everything Will Be Forgotten	35
7. School Starts	39
8. Hans	43
9. The Kinder Joy Egg	47
10. When The Birds Stop Singing	53
11. Jesus My Friend	63
12. The Wall	71
13. Plan B	81

PART 2
14. Men In My Room II	89
15. Treblinka	93
16. Remember Me	99
17. The New Truth	109
18. Ganging Up	115
19. Touching The World Outside	123
20. Ypres	131
21. She Is Gone	139

PART 3
22. Mom Left Long Ago	147
23. How To Free Rapunzel	153
24. Searching For Options	157
25. A House Of Secrets	163
26. The Bystander	169

27. On My Own	173
28. Satan Will Get You	179
29. Angela	185
30. Fighting For Love	189
31. She Is Gone II	193
32. Freeing Rapunzel	199
33. L'Shana Haba'ah B'Yerushalayim (Auf Wiedersehen in Jerusalem)	203
34. Medals	213
Epilogue	225
Acknowledgments	231
About the Author	233

PROLOGUE

Santa Monica, California

"Anne, I just don't know. I don't feel like his mother. I can't do this job."

I hold the cell phone to my ear. On the other end of the line is a woman, Tara, who has recently come to me for life coaching. I listen to her choked sobs, the high-pitched wails of a three-week old infant creating the background soundscape.

"Tell me about how you're feeling."

Tara came to me in her third trimester. She had great respect for the change she would soon undergo—from woman to mother, adopting the joys and burdens of full-time caregiving—and wanted to approach the transition from a grounded place. I was impressed with Tara's wisdom and self-awareness. As she gulps for air, my heart reaches out to her.

"When they brought Daniel to me in the hospital, I thought this couldn't be my child. I didn't feel the way I'm supposed to feel." Tara's voice cracks. "He cries and cries and cries, and I can't comfort him the way a mother should. I can hold him and rock him, but he senses that I'm lost. So, he keeps crying, and I feel terrible; I think God made a mistake giving him to me, that he should have gone to a woman who could do this better...."

Tara breaks off, gasps for air.

"Breathe. Just breathe."

She breathes in heaving gasps. When Tara has regained herself enough, she continues.

"And it's so strange, Anne. I'm remembering things. Things I haven't thought about in years, that I thought I'd moved past."

The past is never dead. It's not even past. The line from William Faulkner floats through layers of my subconscious. "What kind of things?"

"When my baby sister was born, Mom went crazy with her crying. Crazy." Tara's voice has taken on an ominous tone. "She would put her in the crib too hard. Almost throw her down. I would stand there and watch, terrified. Then Mom would slap me and tell me I had to be quiet . . . at least one of us had to, if she was ever going to sleep." Tara struggles to find breath again. "Yesterday I put Daniel down too hard. He looked shocked and cried right away. I felt terrible. I'm so afraid that I'll do it again. I could feel rage move through me. That rage Mom always had toward my sister and me; it's *in* me. I thought it wasn't. That's what I mean by God making a mistake. God should have put Daniel with another woman, where he could be safe."

Tara dissolves into sobs again.

Compassion fills me as painful memories of my own new motherhood rise to the surface. All nine months of pregnancy with my firstborn son, Ariel, I had wished to be done with it. I swung between ambivalence and excitement and did all the things expecting mothers are supposed to do. I didn't drink or smoke, prepared the nursery, attended childbirth class. The teacher assured all of us with swollen bellies that the endorphins from the excitement of ushering new life into the world would help us deal with the pain. "Once you hold your baby in your arms, you forget about all the pain."

Ariel was born by C-section, after sixteen painful hours of labor in Berlin. When I woke from the anesthesia, a nurse pushed a cart toward me bearing a baby who looked too small to be real.

"That is not my child," I said. "There must be some misunderstanding."

"Yes, it is your child," the nurse replied, looking puzzled. She pointed to the tiniest blue wrist band sticking out of a warm towel. "That is your last name, right?"

I gazed at the wristband, confused and still in a haze of pain from the operation. "That is my last name."

My husband Andreas assured me that this was our child, that he had watched the doctors pull him from my incision. Andreas had held the baby already.

"I thought he would look different." These were the only words I could muster for the life we'd just introduced to the world.

The first three days, Ariel slept in the hospital nursery. I could barely move after the surgery, although once a day I forced myself to get up. My son had to be handed to me. At night the nurses took care of him; I couldn't sleep, and the new level of exhaustion overwhelmed me. I cried, awake in bed. I was so tired; how could I take care of my child? For every day from now on? The responsibility almost suffocated me. Darkness nipped at the edges of my bed; I felt my life slipping away.

When we finally came home, my mother-in-law assured me over the phone: "You will grow into motherhood." But I didn't feel myself growing into the role. I didn't feel how the books told me I would feel. Those magical endorphins the childbirth instructor had promised . . . where were they? My parents offered no comfort; they gave Andreas and I the silent treatment, upset because of the name we had chosen for our son.

3

I didn't talk to Andreas about my concerns, afraid he would blame me since I was the one who had pushed us into having children. Anyway, he was going back to work. His company was soon to go public, and Andreas prepared the launch. How I envied his reentry into normal life when my normal life had been stripped away. I felt like I'd died. One day an overwhelming loneliness overcame me, again, when I held Ariel and stared into his little eyes. Tears streamed down my face. "I don't know how to be a good mother to you. I don't know what the future will bring. But I want you to live a happy life."

I was utterly helpless; could Ariel understand? I wanted him to, in some ancient part of himself.

The first few months of Ariel's life, I rarely went out. It was a Berliner winter, and I was overwhelmed at the prospect of protecting him from the cold. I hid in my home. Ariel and I went for the occasional weekend stroll; for the rest of the day, we waited out the hours until Andreas came home. Andreas, my only connection to the outside world.

Some days with Ariel were all right. He would sleep late, and Andreas would proceed as we had in our "before" life: sleeping in, enjoying a long breakfast, and reading the newspaper. On other days, the isolation and endless responsibilities of motherhood became too much. One day, a clear image presented itself: me, with a gun to my head. I could *feel* it—the weight of the pistol in my hand, the cold metal against my forehead, the easy click of the trigger. The scene felt as vivid as if it played before my eyes in that moment. It terrified me.

"I didn't know I still had all these *feelings*," says Tara. "I thought I was doing okay."

"When we meet our children, we meet the best and worst parts of ourselves," I answer. "It's so much more than we bargain for."

Having a child introduced me to my capacity for rage. One day, when Ariel was four, right after our move to California, he drew on the walls of the home we rented. I'd asked him not to do this, as I was worried about angering the owner and having to pay money, which Andreas and I had in short supply.

And I was isolated. I didn't know my neighbors; I didn't know anyone who shared our German culture. I took Ariel's neck in my hands and squeezed. I bent his four-year-old neck back until he sobbed and screamed. By then, Ariel had a two-year-old brother, Tim; I'd locked him up in the other room, and he begged me to stop, distressed by his brother's crying outside his bedroom. Ariel said he was sorry—I wouldn't relent until he did.

A monster had taken over me. When the monster left, every ounce of me filled with shame and horror. Had that really been me? It had been; I sobbed at the realization. In me was the same fury I had seen in my father's eyes, when he'd beaten me or my sisters for some small infraction. I had inflicted the same trauma that was inflicted on me. I needed help.

I hear my client's soft cries on the other end of the line.

"Tara. I think you need to speak to someone."

"That's why I'm speaking to you," she whimpers.

"Not me. At least, not yet." I breathe deeply, choosing my words carefully. "Life coaching is all about the present moment and about the future. You can't make peace with the present moment until you make peace with your past. Have you ever heard of the term 'traumatic reenactment?'"

"I haven't."

"We reenact things to resolve traumas from our past. These reenactments can come in the form of intrusive, compulsive thoughts, or repeated behaviors. It's not pleasant, but the thoughts alert us to something within that needs to be healed."

I can almost feel Tara hold her breath.

"Childbirth can bring up things from our past. Traumas

we'd forgotten about or stuffed down. I know it did for me. I couldn't move forward as the parent my sons needed until I'd faced the past."

Tara exhales slowly. "What are you suggesting? Therapy?"

"I think that would be a good idea. We can continue our work together once you can be present. Right now, you're reliving difficulties from your childhood and anxious about the future. I know how it is. The first months after a baby born can be harder than anyone prepares us for."

"I didn't know it would be like this." Tara cries again. "Maybe if I had known—"

"Listen." It's important that Tara hears this: "You are doing the right thing. You haven't made a mistake. Once you get the help you need, you will be able to show up for your baby and yourself. We *all* need help. The hurts of the past . . . we don't know how they grip us until a traumatic life event makes them rush to the surface."

"I feel terrible that my baby's birth was traumatic!" Tara cries. "I thought it was supposed to be joyful."

"It can be both. Life is paradoxical. That's why it's interesting."

Tara and I chat a little more. When I hang up the phone, I send a silent prayer that she will get the help she needs. *May she find a guide.* Someone who can help Tara confront her painful past and integrate it into her personhood. May the past release its grip and no longer threaten her; may she move forward and remain true to herself, no matter what gets excised from her life in the painful confrontation of her history.

I had wished the same for myself. My own journey—in which I've sought to confront and integrate the painful realities of growing up under the shadow of a man haunted by his past and a woman unable to break free from his controlling grasp—has taken me from my girlhood in Berlin to my adulthood in Santa Monica. I've faced the truth of my family's dark history.

I've sought to understand how Father contorted the wills of the women around him until they bent to his; how my sisters and mother and I squabbled for his love and turned on one another; how we were captives of someone so volatile, frequently drunk, violent, and demeaning.

Mine is a story of abuse within a household that echoed the abuse one nation, Germany, inflicted on a continent—on the world. It is the story of scales falling away from eyes, of seeing the past as it happened and understanding my family's participation in it. At times, I would have traded everything to keep my innocence, to hold onto the world of my childhood which Father built. In this world, he knew best and could set order to his tumultuous past. But as Albert Einstein once said: "The important thing is to not stop questioning." My childhood gave me many questions to unravel and truths to uncover. Before I could see it for what it was and break free, the process of liberation nearly cost me my life.

Yet I lived. I went on to find a life outside my father's home: to go to college and graduate, fall in love, move across continents, and build a new life in a new land. In this life I've become a mother, a friend, a teacher, a school co-founder—and now a life coach. I lived to tell my story.

This is it.

PART 1

1 MEN IN MY ROOM

West Berlin, Germany 1970

I sense them before I see them.

Men—at least three—are in my room, hiding. They stand at attention and answer to a master who is invisible to me. Eventually, the men come into focus. Although I don't dare open my eyes, I can picture their gray uniforms, the dark sticks they hold. They are after me. I pull my blanket over my face and play dead. If the men see me, they will kill me.

The men creep closer to my bed. Where is Bello, my stuffed dog? I move my arm carefully and quietly, hoping it will land on his soft fur.

I am four and alone. My sisters, twins who are two years older than I, sleep together downstairs. I long for a companion to share my terror and perhaps lessen it as the men advance.

My mind gives my body silent directions: *Be quiet! Don't move! Hold your breath!*

I try to obey, clenching every muscle and risking only the tiniest sips of air.

A cracking sound—a plank shifts underneath the green carpet of my room. The men are still here. Under the blanket, it is difficult to breathe. Yet I know I must risk breath and discovery if I'm to escape the men and the certain death they bring.

My Aunt Anna has come from Bavaria and is in the next room. I must go to her. As quietly as I can, I whip the covers off my bed and stand.

Be quiet! Screams the voice in my head.

Like Bello, I prick my ears up to hear the slightest movement. But they only ring in the silence. The men are ready to pounce when I attempt my escape—I sense it.

I force myself to open my squeezed-shut eyes. Across from my bed, I make out the outline of a cabinet. There—that is where one of the men hides, in the gap between the cabinet and the wall. I must be fast. When I've summoned enough courage, I bolt.

But my legs have become leaden. I force myself and take three giant steps to the door. Just one more move, and then I will be free.

I am too exposed here. I push down the handle to my door. It is strange that the door is closed, since I always leave it open—they are watching me; they are coming—but wait. I shudder when the handle refuses to budge after another jostle. Tonight, the door is locked.

Furious tears sting the back on my eyes. I fall to my knees in search of the key—it must be here somewhere. I fumble in the dark, desperate for my hands to close over the tiny piece of metal that will save me from the men's sticks. My hands find only carpet.

No!

"Aunt Anna," I call, my voice tiny with terror. No answer.

"Aunt Anna." This time I force more air through my lungs, risk the men discovering me. Still, my aunt doesn't come.

"Aunt Anna!" I scream, shaking with terror. The tears that sting the backs of my eyes threaten to overtake me.

"Wahggie?"

At the sound of Aunt Anna's nonsense nickname for me, something releases inside my chest. Her footsteps shuffle in the hallway, and the torrent of tears I have been storing releases.

"I am so frightened," I sob. "I want to get out."

"Mmmm." Aunt Anna rattles the door but cannot open it either. I sink against the wall as more sobs escape me.

"I can't find the key, Wahggie. It is locked."

A small panel of wood separates me and the men from Aunt Anna. I wish I could tear it down, but I feel my strength slip away.

"Turn on the light, Wahggie."

Although it will expose me to the men, I have no choice. I flip the switch; light floods my room. I stand with my back to the wall, then slide slowly down. My legs are still so weak. The silent tears fall.

I blink back the wetness and watch for the men, but they have disappeared. Instead, I see stuffed animals looking at me from their shelf. I see my picture books. Across from me is my red wooden toy shop, standing there like nothing has happened. Moment by moment, the truth settles in. A dream—that's all it was. But as my breath returns, the fear remains.

"I will be back in a minute," Aunt Anna whispers. I hear her climbing down the stairs.

Why was the door locked? I hope Aunt Anna will be back soon. The minutes seem to drag on as I stand behind my door, waiting.

After an eternity, I hear Aunt Anna mountain the stairs, arguing with Mother. I understand fragments of what she says. "How can you lock her up" and "irresponsible...."

A key is inserted into the lock. Mother enters my room. She stands, lit by the hallway light in her short nightgown, her arms and legs menacing in their nakedness. Her dark eyes are fixed on me.

"What is all the fuss about?" Mother demands.

I feel stupid now, under the bright lights in my room.

"When I was as young as you are now, I had to stay in my room even when we heard the bombs dropping," Mother says. I can tell by the slant of her eyebrows that she is furious. "You must overcome your fears. You cannot bother people at night, especially not Aunt Anna."

My face burns; I am ashamed to be the source of so much confusion. Aunt Anna clutches the key; she does not turn it over to Mother. My aunt shakes her head, thin white ponytail resting over her shoulder, and draws her nightgown around her. When Mother stomps downstairs to her own room, Aunt Anna turns her gaze to me.

"Come." She holds out her hand to me, and I follow my aunt into her bedroom with a sigh of relief. When she holds up the blanket in her bed, I gladly slip in beside her. I inhale Aunt Anna's perfume. Elsa and Gerda, my sisters, don't want to get too close to Aunt Anna: she is old, nearly eighty, as Father has told us. But I am grateful for her closeness, her warmth. We are accomplices. I help Aunt Anna navigate around our neighborhood since our city, Berlin, is not familiar to her. I enjoy the feel of my hand in hers, how I can help her walk since her ancient knees are always sore. And now she has saved me from the men.

And Mother.

"Thank you," I whisper to Aunt Anna. She turns and in moments snores softly. Heaviness overtakes me. Where is Bello?

I have left my stuffed dog in my room—but I will not leave Aunt Anna's side until morning. My breath falls in rhythm with hers. For now, I am safe; I have a friend to stay with me in this house, an ally against the dangers of the night and those that come with the morning.

Sleep embraces me; I finally give in.

2 LIKE RAPUNZEL IN THE TOWER

I cannot explain to Mother about the men in gray uniforms. "Forget about these dreams!" she says, shaking her head in dismay, as though I would make it up. In the same way I cannot explain to her why I do not want to go to her bedroom. Mother and Father's bedroom always smells sour sweet, like a glass of dill pickles. What's more, Mother's touch does not comfort me. I recoil at it. In any case, I have been placed on the third floor so I will not bother my parents.

As I once overheard Father say to Mother: "Babies have to scream through the night. It is better not to listen. They will stop eventually. I don't want them to become spoiled tyrants."

This is Father's philosophy, and Mother agrees. Why should I accept her offer of comfort now?

I feel that Father and Mother handle me differently from Elsa and Gerda, my twin sisters, born two years earlier than me. At least Elsa and Gerda have the fact of their twin-ness to speak for them. Wherever they go, they are a spectacle. They are lively, bright, and confident; family and strangers alike love to marvel at how similar they look. At least they were grateful that I was born. I was an extra playmate for them;

someone on whom they could lavish attention when the mood struck. In an early black and white picture, they are dressed alike and cradling me. They look down at me and smile as I smile, secure in their affection. I love and admire them, too, though I can never inhabit the special world of their making.

Gerda was born first, ten minutes before Elsa. Even now, it is all about who is first:

I am four, trying desperately to keep up with Elsa and Gerda as they fly down the streets of Berlin to Messelpark. Their shoulder-length brown braids flutter like flags in the wind as they round a corner and disappear. Like always, I am far behind. Aunt Anna calls out pointlessly: "Slow down! Not so fast!"

When I arrive at the playground out of breath, Elsa and Gerda are already climbing up the play structure. I hear Elsa crowing on the top: "First!" Her blue eyes sparkle proudly.

Everyone wants to play with my sisters. They remind me of my wind-up dog, except that they never stop: who can swing the highest, who can dangle upside down the longest, who is the last one holding on to the roundabout. They are my heroines. Wherever we go, they get long looks from strangers. Mom beams when she is asked:

"They are adorable! How do you keep them apart?"

I want to be with them all the time. At night when the nightmares are coming back, I sneak down from my third-story bedroom to their shared bedroom on the second floor. But Mother is not happy with this. One day as I play in my room with my doll kitchen, she enters.

"Your father and I want you to learn to be on your own. You cannot spend all your time with your sisters. They are twins; they have to stay together. I am tired of you crawling in other people's beds at night."

Mother's voice softens. "Look at how nice your bedroom is.

And as I've told you before, you may come into *my* bedroom if you are scared."

But I continue to take my chances and sneak to the second floor, taking refuge in Elsa and Gerda's room. On lucky nights, I can stay there until morning without discovery. Many times, I am caught. When I hear Mother approaching, I hide as quickly as I can, behind the door or under the bed. Sometimes my sisters betray me; sometimes they don't. But the sight of me in my sisters' bedroom never fails to send Mother into a fury. If she is armed with a hanger, I pray harder that I can stay concealed from her gaze.

When Mother catches me careening up the stairs, she holds me by the wrists, pressing them against each other with one hand and trying to hit me with the other. We become locked in a strange dance on the staircase; she one step beneath me, me wrestling to free myself and fly up the remaining steps. Gerda and Elsa watch, but I don't see them. I am too busy trying to escape—an antelope desperate to shake off the lioness's claw.

At least I feel safer when Aunt Anna or Omi Dina stay with us in the room next to mine. Omi Dina, Mother's mother, brushes her long gray hair over the room's small sink before twisting it artfully into a bun. She is beautiful; Mother resembles her. On slow mornings, my sisters and I crawl into Omi Dina's bed. She tells us stories from her childhood.

There was a great war, Omi says, and then another big one. Omi had to flee from her hometown on an old cart with her sister and mom. They fled the bad guys—the Russians. Father's father, my grandpa, had died in the first big war. That is why I never met him, and perhaps why Omi Marie, Father's mother, looked sick from sadness when I met her one Christmas in the old people's home.

It is not only Omi's war stories that I like so much. She also reads me good night fairy tales, sitting on my bed until I fall asleep.

"Today, I read you about Rapunzel." She says, puts her glasses on, and leans over the book. And I hear the tale for the first time. The story of the beautiful girl who is captured by the witch in the tower, waiting for the prince to free her, fascinates me.

"I would like to have that long, thick blond hair," I say quietly, staring at the ceiling. Omi closes the book, kisses me, and smiles.

"Good night," she says.

"Good night," I reply.

The story stays with me, and I imagine how I would throw my thick blond hair out my window and watch it fall down past my sisters' room and my mother's study before hitting the ground. Hans, our new neighbor, could climb up and play with me in my room—a playmate of my very own. Perhaps then I would not escape so often into Gerda and Elsa's room.

The fantasy makes me smile—but then I run my fingers through my very short hair, kept how Mother likes it.

Perhaps there is another way for Rapunzel to be free.

3   BETRAYAL

My sisters and I hardly ever see Father. He is an important man, the head of a hospital in Berlin. He spends his days in the hospital, nurses and doctors scurrying around him and answering to his every whim. In the evenings, he disappears in his study with books and medical journals. A cloud of cigar smoke engulfs Father's heavy desk, a single lamp illuminating him. Or Father entertains guests, our home filled with musicians, doctors, and other members of the Berlin elite. I like those evenings, when the house is filled with music and laughter and the comforting smells of roast, spices, and wine mixed with cigarette smoke. I can see how women like Father.

Once in the middle of the night, when I woke up to the sound of the piano, I ran downstairs on tippy-toes and peaked around the corner in our living room. I saw all the women gathered around the grand piano singing a German song, while Father's fingers flew over the keys accompanying them. He looked happy and kind. He shared his seat with one of them, and I could see them all stare at him, smiling their best smiles.

Father never comes to my room on the third floor, except when I am sick. He transforms then into the kind doctor, his eyes mild and gazing only at me. Father cares for me and makes sure I get well as fast as possible. He gives Mother orders to provide me with the right medication. I hang on Father's every word, and he hangs on mine; with his attention fully on me I begin to feel better at once. The closeness is so precious, I don't mind being sick. In times of wellness, Father is a stranger to me—yet his power over the house is absolute.

On an otherwise unremarkable afternoon, Mother bursts into my room.

"Was it you, Anne?" Her eyes are frantic, furious.

Mother holds a pink colored pullover in her hands. I sit on the floor and gaze up at her, not wanting to be bothered. I am playing with my shape sorting cube. I've just finished putting all the shapes into the right holes.

I turn from Mother and open the cube with a blue colored key, taking pleasure in the creaking noise the key makes when I turn it in the keyhole. I now take the colorful shapes out to start all over again.

"Anne, was it you?"

I look up for a moment, then keep my attention on the shape sorting game and try to ignore the prickle of fear at my neck.

"Did you put the red pillow in the washing machine?"

"No." 'Washing machine'—Mother is speaking about grown-up things. I exhale. Someone is guilty of something, but it is not me.

Mother runs downstairs. I hear her ask the same question of Elsa and Gerda, who each say "no." For now, the matter is settled.

I think no more of it until that evening, when Father returns home.

"Your Father would like to talk with you."

The words send a chill through me; I exchange wide-eyed looks with Elsa and Gerda. It is rare that Father summons us.

When he does, it is because a wrong needs to be righted. Someone will be punished—the question is, who.

My sisters and I stand outside the big white door of his study. Nervous, I shift from one foot to the other. It is evening; I have not seen Father since morning when I greeted him in his bedroom, as I do every morning. Mother makes me. I must shake his hand and curtsy; if my greeting is unsatisfactory, I do it again. When my face lets my true feelings about this ritual show—that I find it awkward and embarrassing—Mother pouts. I must be kind to Father, she says. It is what I owe him as his daughter.

Now in front of Father's study Elsa, Gerda, and I look from one to the other. Who should knock?

Gerda raises her hand and raps on the door.

"Come in."

I take a deep breath as Gerda opens the door.

Father's desk lamp illuminates the room the air thick with cigar smoke. While we approach, timid steps on the plush carpet, he writes something in a small notebook. We halt in front of the desk, the three of us in a row facing him. Still Father writes. Finally, he finishes—puts down his pen and looks up, his eyes studying us through dark-framed glasses. He smiles.

I shiver.

When Father finally speaks, his smile stays in place. "I heard that a red pillow was put in the washing machine. I also heard that the remaining white laundry turned pink. Unfortunately, your mother's cashmere pullover is ruined. I want to know who put the pillow into the washing machine."

Red pillow. Washing machine. The grown-up things my mother was so upset about earlier.

"We already asked the housekeepers, but they don't know anything about it," Father continues. "It must have been one of you. I want the one who did it to step forward."

We all stand still. I don't dare to move.

"Mmh." Father exhales through clenched teeth.

I steal glances at Elsa and Gerda and see them staring at me. A brief shiver goes through Gerda's slim body, but she says nothing. Maybe she is cold, as I am cold in my white nighty.

"You must know by now that I hate lies." Father's voice now has an edge. "We don't lie, because if you lie, I cannot trust you anymore. Lying is a sin. You don't lie to your parents."

I cannot see Father's face. I stand in front of the desk light and can make out only his shadow on the desk. Still, I can feel his blue eyes making holes in my body. That is why I don't like to look at him. There is something about his gaze which forces me to look away.

"So, let's see. Gerda. What do you have to say?"

"I don't know. I didn't do it." Gerda's voice sounds wobbly with held-back tears, yet there is also a forced calmness, like she is a lion tamer working to soothe the wild cat. "I don't know how this could happen. I was not in the laundry room."

"Okay, Elsa, what about you?"

"I don't know." She shakes her head, stares into the white carpet. "But I saw Anne there the other day. She is the one on the third floor."

"Me?" I ask. I have not been in the laundry room in several days.

"Yes, you." Elsa nods her head wildly.

"No, I was not. That is not true." Suddenly, I can't remember anything. *Have* I been in the laundry room?

I can feel Father's eyes boring into me like small needles.

"Your room is closest to the laundry room." Father's voice is sharp like a knife.

I lift my head. When I open my mouth, nothing comes out.

"I gather that one of you is lying, definitely," Father continues, apparently unbothered by the lack of a confession.

"You will now come to me, one after the other, and whisper in my ear who it was. It is time to admit your wrongdoing."

He signals that I should be first. He smiles at me, encouraging. I like his smile, but I know what pain it can bring.

Father thinks that I know something, but I still have no idea what all this is about. I approach him and go around the desk. He leans down to me smelling of cigar, his big hand cupping his ear to better listen.

Gerda and Elsa watch me. I can see fear mixed with suspicion in their eyes, the same fear that must be plain in mine. I don't want to say anything, but I must obey. There will be a harsh punishment , I know, for lying. Yet if I disobey and don't give an answer, that will bring punishment too.

Father whispers. "Anne, who was it?" Again, there is his encouraging smile. Father wants me to confess, and *I want* to, just to please him. But to what?

His heavy body blocks the desk light; it is dark when I mutter, "I don't know."

Father shakes his head. Now it is on to Elsa. I see her lips move. Did she give Father my name again? I hope so much that she did not. Or did she also say she didn't know?

My heart races.

Gerda's turn now. Another whisper. I am so scared, I cannot hear what she is saying.

And then it is over. The cigar lies forgotten in the ashtray; the heavy smoke makes breathing difficult.

Father says, "Okay. You can all leave now. I have to make up my mind."

We move out of the room in single file. Outside, we don't talk. I don't dare ask my sisters what they murmured in Father's ear. They don't ask me either.

The uncertainty makes my stomach ache. I go straight upstairs to my room and crawl into bed, though sleep doesn't come until hours later.

The next day, Gerda is in tears. She tells me that she was beaten by Father in the living room.

This time, she is the one who was marked for punishment. How long did Father beat her? How long will the bruises last? All this for a pink sweater. I cannot understand how a pillow in the wash could spawn so much anguish. Still, I clock away the new rules: *never put a pillow in the wash.*

Even with the new rules filed away, even that I know that I am innocent this time, I cannot shake the feeling that Gerda's beating is all my fault.

4 HANDS TELL THE TRUTH

One night, I open my eyes to darkness. There is noise downstairs, a constant murmur. A door smashes; I startle, then get out of bed to see what is going on. I grab Fridolin, my orange rag doll, a gift from Omi Dina. I like his crooked smile, the soft fur which frames his face, and the tiny bell attached to his long orange cap. Fridolin, Bello—I can count on my stuffed toys for comfort.

Two dark figures sit at the top of the staircase. I join Elsa and Gerda, who have been awoken by the clatter too, sitting here for who knows how long. The noise comes from Father and Mother's bedroom. I shiver in the darkness and lean against my sisters.

Father's loud voice booms: "What do you want? You have a gardener and two housekeepers. And *I* pay them."

I can't understand Mother's reply, though I hear her screaming and crying. Father laughs wildly; things crash and fall on the floor, and I jump on the stair. Though I am only in preschool, I begin to understand the content of the fight. Mother has asked for more money, and Father doesn't want to give it.

Gerda shakes her head. Elsa leans forward to listen better.

I must know more. "What is it about?" I whisper into Gerda's ear, but my sister shrugs her shoulder and puts an index finger to her mouth. Finally, the lights go out, and the noise quiets.

As I climb back up to my room, I wonder how things will be different in the morning. What price we might all have to pay.

The next day, Mother and Father drive me to preschool. Mom explains that she needs the car and will drive Father to work after they have dropped me off. Now Father is driving; he is in a very bad mood. Father explains, slowly enough that his youngest daughter can understand, that Mom did something wrong when guests were at our house the other day.

Snatches of Father's shouts from the night before come back to me. "How can you embarrass me in front of all the guests by not following my orders? You better make sure you do it next time!" And "I won't give you more money."

What did Mother do and not do?

On the drive to preschool, the knife's edge in Father's voice scares me. It seems as if he could explode any minute. Mother makes no reply to Father's accusations, just sits in front of me and stares silently ahead. I feel her sadness creeping through the seat into me; I want to protect her, as I had longed to protect Gerda after her beating.

I offer Mom my hand. It slips through the gap of the passenger's seat; now I can touch Mother without Father's notice. I don't know how to help, but I want her to know that I am here.

My hand finds Mom's hand; she pets it. *I am so sad; help me,* the hand seems to say. But also, *you are too small; you don't understand.* I don't recoil at her touch the way I do when she offers to comfort me after my night terrors. It is easier for me to give her comfort.

The car stops in front of the preschool, a friendly building made of red bricks. I swallow a lump in my throat, open the rear door, and leave the sadness of my parents' car.

After preschool, I take the double-decker bus home. It is my first time riding on my own, though I took practice rides with Elsa and Gerda throughout the summer. In Germany, it is not uncommon for children as young as almost five to ride on the bus alone, but I am the youngest person on the bus by many years. I climb the bus's steps, my chest swelling with fear and pride.

"Where is your mom?" the driver asks, unsmiling.

I don't know what to say, so I shake my head instead of speaking, then give him the twenty Pfennig and sit right behind him. I will mind my own business. I will not speak to strangers, as Elsa and Gerda have taught me. I grip the edge of my seat as the bus sails down the city streets, then comes to a stop several blocks from my house. As I climb my front steps, I grin from ear to ear. I have done it. My first bus ride all alone.

When Mom opens the door, her face is all order and ordinariness. There is no trace of the sadness of the morning's car ride—of the special language our hands communicated to one another outside Father's gaze. Instead, Mother ushers me inside like nothing extraordinary has happened at all.

A vague feeling of disappointment settles over me as I cross the threshold. Some part of me had hoped our closeness in the car would continue in the home. Our hands had told the truth; couldn't we speak the truth as well? What had happened between her and Father the night before? What was the bad thing she had done? Couldn't I know, so as not to repeat her mistake? Was all well again?

But there would be no talk of this. An uneasy peace settles over the house again; now we must all try not to break it.

The trouble is, I never know what the breaking point will be.

5 NURSE

Father's temper and Mother's response to it—or lack thereof—is the backdrop against which my sisters and I live. I make note of the spoken and unspoken rules—*no red pillows in the wash, no asking for more than you deserve, and no sneaking to see my sisters in the nighttime*—then try my best to stay within the invisible lines drawn, since crossing one could result in a beating or days of quiet anger. In the same way, my parents' pleasure comes as a happy surprise. I seize upon their affection and determine to pin it down. One day, I stumble upon an ambition of which Mother approves.

My sisters and I are invited to our neighbor's house one day, the Draches. When we arrive, we find Mr. and Mrs. Drache outstretched in loungers in their huge backyard. I am embarrassed by the sight of Ms. Drache in her swimming suit, Mr. Drache in his trunks. They are both so tan and good-looking, their smiles dazzling. Mother says Mr. Drache is a famous movie star, and I believe her. Still, I cannot help but view the Draches as I imagine my parents would. How much time must they spend lying here? Are they lazy?

Laziness—something my father despises. When Father is

home, he is doing either: practicing his violin, studying in the office, entertaining friends, reading the newspaper. On Sunday morning our family takes long trips to the forest to hike or bike. Lying on a lounger in the backyard—I can't even picture my parents doing this.

My sisters and I kick a plastic ball with the Drache's daughter, Nicki. Then we jump into the wonderful cold water of their inflatable paddling pool. If this is laziness, I think there is something to be said for it.

When I've had enough of splashing, I climb out of the water and become aware of Mr. Drache observing me. I wrap myself in an impossibly thick, warm towel.

Mr. Drache asks,

"Anne, do you know what your father is doing?"

What a weird question. Of course I know.

"He is a doctor," I answer matter-of-factly.

"Okay. And what is he doing the whole day?"

This question I cannot answer so easily. Mr. and Mrs. Drache peer at me, Mrs. Drache's hair a main of white. Big round sunglasses take up her entire face; I study her nose, which reminds me of an eagle's beak.

I think. Two days ago, Mom and I had visited Father at the hospital. A woman picked us up from the parking lot; Mom had explained that she was father's secretary. The secretary brought us to his room. Father in his chair behind a huge wooden desk, reading a newspaper, just as he did at home.

"I know what Father is doing," I answer at last.

"What?" Mr. Drache asks.

"He is reading newspapers."

Mr. and Mrs. Drache double over with laughter that lasts for a small eternity. What have I said that is so funny? When Mr. Drache catches his breath and wipes a tear from his eye, he has yet another question for me.

"And what do you want to do later in life?"

Will my answer make them laugh again? I hesitate. "A doctor."

"Then you will have to read too many newspapers!" Mr. Drache exclaims. "I think a nurse would suit you better."

"And what does a nurse do?"

I glance behind me. Elsa, Gerda, and Nicki have taken their seats behind us on the lawn and listen quietly to our conversation. It is a beautiful day, and the sun warms my cool skin. I enjoy being the center of attention.

Gerda's voice comes from behind me. "Don't you remember Christmas Eve at the hospital with the nurses?"

I recall that wonderful day—the sisters in their gray smocks and small white box-shaped caps attached to their hair. I held hands with one and balanced a candlestick in my other hand. The head nurse and I led the group, singing beautiful Christmas songs while walking through the halls of the hospital. We went upstairs, downstairs from hallway to hallway, singing for the sick people.

Even now, I can hear the wonderful sound of the nurses' high, clear voices echoing from the walls. I can almost smell the fire from the candlesticks, mixed with the fragrant needles Christmas trees decorated with ornaments and more candles—two in each hallway.

"Yes, I want to become a nurse," I say, more confidently this time.

"Wonderful." Mr. Drache beams. "Then you can help the patients and see that they feel better soon."

He later takes a picture of me with a big silver camera.

Back at home and in preschool, I tell everyone I want to become a nurse. This excites Mom. She buys me a nurse costume: a white smock and white scarf for over my hair, emblazoned with a small red cross. I really love it and show off my get-up proudly.

Mom takes a picture of me laughing and clapping excitedly

on the dark green staircase. I think of how lucky I am to have discovered this path that pleases the grown-ups in my life so greatly.

What I don't see then is how the world around me upholds an order in which men are dominant. Certainly, I notice this pattern in my own home; Mother does whatever is necessary to please Father, rushing around to placate his every disgruntlement, just as the hospital staff does. I later come to understand that Mother is highly educated—she has a Ph.D. Still, the man is dominant, and the measure of a woman is how well she can keep a home and serve him. If I had persisted in the wish to be a doctor that day in the Drache's backyard, would Mr. Drache have smiled so easily? Would Mother have purchased a doctor costume and taken my picture, a rare smile lightening her face?

I do not know. For now, all I know is a four-year-old's delight in her mother's smile. I wish to live in this moment always.

6 WHEN YOU GET MARRIED, EVERYTHING WILL BE FORGOTTEN

By 1972, I have learned how to read. Though I still long for a companion of my own—someone with whom to share the closeness my sisters take for granted—the books offer welcome escape. Within their pages, I can forget Father's rages, Mom's sadness, how Elsa and Gerda delight in ratting me out to our parents for whatever infraction I may have committed. I fall into the stories of Snow White, Little Red Riding Hood, and my early favorite, Rapunzel.

When Aunt Anna visits, I rejoice, because I now have her on the third floor with me and feel more at ease. We read to each other. Aunt Anna encourages me as she folds clean clothes in the small laundry room with the sloping roof, air thick with steam. "Make Snow White sound softer," she says, "and the wolf in Little Red Riding Hood more dangerous." I try my best, reading to Aunt Anna as she sighs and wipes a white strand of hair from her wrinkled face, the mountain of laundry before her. After she is done, Aunt Anna falls back into her armchair in her room next to mine.

I know that she is very tired—she has just turned eighty.

Still, I am grateful that Aunt Anna has come to look after my sisters and me. I can always count on her kindness.

I wander over to Aunt Anna, biting my lip. I must show her something.

The other day I had woken up early, giddy with excitement about celebrating Carnival at school. Carnival happens right before Lent, a grand party full of silliness and fun before the somber days of fasting. In the early morning hours, I'd donned my white princess dress, a small golden crown attached to my head with a rubber band. I couldn't contain myself. Up and down the hallways I ran at 6:00 in the morning, the sky still black—until Father caught me and pulled down my tights. He hit me—hard—on my bum, over and over again, before leaving me in the dark.

It was far from the first time I'd been beaten. Once I was beaten for picking the apples off our tree in the backyard too soon. Another happened after I playfully kneeled in the road, showing Elsa and Gerda that it was safe—no cars were coming. Elsa and Gerda had told on me as soon as we'd burst through the front door, savoring their power. My punishment had come, swift and severe.

"Look what Father did to me," I tell Aunt Anna, sniffling and showing her the bruises on my bum.

"Oh my," says Aunt Anna, confirming what I believed to be true: *this is very bad. Fathers should not do this to their children.* Certainly, Aunt Anna would "blow the hurt away," a common way to soothe boo-boos in Germany.

"When you get married, everything will be forgotten." She smiles.

Aunt Anna's words bewilder me. When I get *married*? What does getting married have to do with Father's beating me?

I brood over the question, turn it over in my mind the next several weeks. Does getting married magically erase past hurts? Does each girl carry a history of pain, wiped out on her wedding day? Is this true of Mrs. Drache—what dark secrets lie in her past, beneath the glamour she wears so easily? Is this true of Aunt Anna? And if it is true for Mother, then why does she still wear her sadness as heavily as a winter coat?

I think of Rapunzel alone in her tower. How I long for her to be free, to leave the darkness of the tower and start over with her prince. "Everything will be forgotten." Such a promise seems impossible, and yet I have no reason to doubt Aunt Anna, who's as good a friend as I can hope for.

The words burrow deep within me. They will change me in ways I can only now see with the benefit of hindsight. I will return to them again and again, throughout a tumultuous and isolating adolescence—the promise of oblivion, of beginning as someone else.

I settle against Aunt Anna as her words settle inside me, changing me for better and for worse.

7 SCHOOL STARTS

Thanks to Aunt Anna, I am an early reader. I am one of the few who know how to read when I begin school in 1972. On the evening of the first day of school, Father calls me into his study. I hesitate before entering—is he angry? What could Father want from me?

But Father is smiling. He pulls something from behind his back: a stuffed animal fox with orange fur, white snout, and black whiskers.

"I want you to be as smart as this fox right here," says Father.

I take the fox into my arms, my heart a mix of pride and worry. I am delighted that Father has given me this special present and am determined to do my best in school. Yet what if I am not as smart as the fox? What if I fail to make my teachers happy, as I so often fail my parents?

But my worries melt away at school, which I enjoy right away. I like my teacher, Frau Schneider, with her large, brown-rimmed glasses that remind me of an owl. Frau Schneider yells at other students when they don't listen or follow directions quickly enough, but she likes me.

When I look back later in life, I wonder if Frau Schneider took to me because of my skills or because of my father. She respected Father and the place he held in society; Frau Schneider even became his patient years later. Father's shadow looms large. The older I get, the more I see that there is no place in my life his shadow does not reach.

As much as I take pleasure in school, I can't help but feel guilty about how Elsa and Gerda struggle academically. They are two years ahead of me and struggle to read and write. One afternoon, my mother shows me letters that Elsa and Gerda have written to Omi Dina and Opi. My grandparents have corrected my sisters' errors with a red pen. I'm surprised by how the red bleeds across the page, glaring and ugly.

During one Sunday lunch, the word 'dyslexia' comes up in relation to my sisters. My mother looks down at the table with her lips squeezed together, and I think dyslexia must be a very bad disease. The word hardens something within my father.

"Dyslexia didn't exist during my childhood," Father states matter-of-factly. "My mother just hit my cousin with a ruler every time she misspelled a word. It was amazing to see how fast she got cured."

Elsa, Gerda, Mother, and I avoid Father's gaze as he casually eats a spoonful of mashed potatoes.

I file away the lesson. *Don't get dyslexia. Continue to do well with writing to avoid a beating.* At the same time, I feel guilty that I cannot protect Elsa and Gerda from the disease and the punishment.

Still, I cannot help my pride that in this one regard I outshine Elsa and Gerda. I even become cocky and enjoy my sisters' anger when I come home with a perfect grade. But my joy turns to sadness when they give me the cold shoulder. If I allow myself to become better than Elsa and Gerda, I risk that they don't like me anymore.

Father does not help; he uses me as an example to show

how mediocre my sisters are. He quizzes them on spelling words; when they do not answer correctly, Father asks me. I spell the word correctly, and Father beams, a cold glint in his eye.

"See? I knew you were smarter."

I warm to Father's attention; at the same time, I wish I could hide from him and the never-ending contest of "who's best" waged among the girls in my family. The "winner" changes so quickly: Elsa one day, Gerda another, me the next. No one is safe on the pedestal; a mistake can knock you off until Father gives his favor once again.

As for Mother, who is so much younger than Father that he acts as her teacher, treats her as one of his daughters in need of correction. Father rarely acknowledges when Mother does something right. In his presence, she acts like a dog waiting for treats to be thrown her way. Mother can never win Father's approval, no matter what she does. While each of her daughters may take a moment on the winner's podium, Father always keeps her away from the stand. Sometimes he recruits his daughters in Mother's humiliation.

The only one exempt from the game is Father. By virtue of being a man, he sits above the fray. Father has nothing to prove; he makes the game and sets the players against one another. He is the one who decides.

He is the one who decides.

8 HANS

I love school, and in the afternoons, I like to play with my classmate and neighbor, Hans. We sit next to each other in first grade. Hans is much taller than I, with black hair, a gaunt face, strong nose, and dark brown sparkling eyes. His family came from Bremen and moved into the house next to ours when I was five. Hans is my friend.

We mostly play at his house—my house is too uncomfortable, my room too small, and the living room too big and rigid. But Hans and I prefer to play outside anyway, dangling our legs and letting out shrieks as we go up and down, up and down on the seesaw in my backyard. Most often, Hans and I prefer to hide in the soft lilac bushes on the side of the terrace, the strong fragrance tingling our noses. We pluck the panicles of the light purple flowers, enjoying the taste of honey. Or we dig deep holes in the sandbox his father built in the middle of their backyard.

Hans has the right equipment—spates, shovels, buckets, and diggers. It's everything we need to create sandcastles, tunnels, and roads for our cars. By the sandbox is a stone well. We lower our buckets down into its depths and struggle with heavy loads of water, then pour them into our lagoons and castle moats. Hans always has the best ideas for what to build—the castles can never be high enough nor the tunnels long enough to suit him. I love the sound the shovel makes as it glides into the packed sand, like the sound of the spray a wave makes after it crashes on the beach.

Hans' backyard is a paradise—surrounded by trees and beautiful flowers which his mother tends. It holds treasure; we are sure of it. Sometimes, Hans and I dig for oil beneath the sand. We know how precious oil is: due to the oil crisis Father and Mother keep talking about, no one is allowed to use their cars on Sundays. We dig so deep that we hit black dirt beneath the sand, which makes Hans' father angry. He is an engineer and likes everything just so. But the black dirt confirms that we are on the right path, inches from liquid fortune. We dig deeper; we will find it and live like kings.

While Hans may rule outside, inside I am in charge. We play Teacher in his playroom. I am thrilled by the large magnetic easel with colorful letters, the green chalk board. Here I play Mrs. Schneider; Hans is my pupil. I make him arrange the letters into words on the easel. When Hans loses interest in the game, I yell at him, exactly like Mrs. Schneider does. Hans tires of me scolding him and always asks if *he* can be the teacher—which is obviously not possible, since Mrs. Schneider is a *girl* and Hans is a boy. Eventually though, I relent. Hans can be Mr. Coin, our math teacher.

Sometimes my angry Mrs. Schneider screams draw Hans' mother to the playroom. "Is everything all right?" she asks.

For me, everything is perfect. Screaming is how adults get what they want, so I rage at Hans and tell him what to do. But I am not upset. I would rather be with Hans than anywhere else.

My parents don't always share my warm view of Hans' family. They don't have a nanny, a cook, or a gardener. My mother calls them "misers," unwilling to spend what is necessary to keep up a household. Our neighbors the Draches are lazy; Hans' family are misers. Just as we inside the home can never please Mother and Father, it appears that our neighbors always fall short of my parents' favor too.

    I do my best to ignore my parents' comments. With Hans, I have what Elsa and Gerda have—a companion. He doesn't care about pleasing Father or ratting me out for my mistakes. He is a friend of my very own; with him, I am safe.

9 THE KINDER JOY EGG

One day after school in third grade, Hans holds out a handful of money toward me.

"Come on, let's go to Martin's Bakery. I want to spend some of my allowance."

Martin's Bakery is our favorite. It is chock-full of tempting treats, delicious pastries displayed neatly in glass cabinets and fragrant with the smell of sugar mixed with coffee and chocolate. On the left-hand side of the store are dozens of treats you can buy for only one Pfennig—candy, licorice, gummy bears, and fizzy tablets. I head to Martin's first thing each Saturday after I get my allowance and pick the most delicious candy from the bins.

"Race you!" I say.

I run as fast as I can. I want to be a tomboy; I love wearing pants and like my short hair now. When people address me in stores with, "What can I do for you, young man?" I feel proud, especially in the presence of Hans. I am always trying to prove to him that even though I am a girl, I can do everything boys can do.

We tear down the street toward Martin's. We are both eager

to see its newest treasure—the Kinder Joy egg. It is brand new and so popular it is often sold out. The bakery owners display it proudly in the center of the counter; young children jump up and try to grab it. Who can blame them? The eggs are marvelous, wrapped in shiny orange tin foil. My classmates and I hold competitions to see who can peel off the foil in one piece.

Once the peeling is done—*aha*. The chocolate appears, smelling wonderful, of cacao mixed with milk and sugar. The egg is made of two thin wafers which must be separated very carefully. When I bite the chocolate, it makes a gentle clicking sound; once on my tongue, the chocolate melts in my mouth. Inside the chocolate egg is another egg, this one yellow and plastic—inside that, a surprise. Sometimes it is a little action figure, sometimes a car or a puppet; it could be anything tiny that is guaranteed to give you at least an hour of joy, as the magic egg's name suggests.

After school the bakery is crowded—it is a small space, and five people inside make the store feel packed. Hans and I wait patiently in line. Then, Hans shoots me a mischievous look. He grabs an egg from the counter and places it in his pocket.

My breath catches. With a pretend nonchalance, Hans places it back. But then a few moments later, the look returns into his eyes, and he does it again.

Hans glances at me with a cocked eyebrow. I read the challenge in his expression. *Can you do it? Are you brave enough?*

I glance ahead to the counter; the shopkeepers are busy with the other customers. Following Hans' lead, I move my hand to the shelf. I take an egg and place it in my pocket, then put it back.

He takes one, puts it in his pocket, then places it back.

I take one, put it in my pocket. I leave it there.

In the moment, I feel only excitement. I have risen to Hans' game—proven my worth and my courage. A devilish joy spreads through me—the joy of not getting caught.

"Next!" Calls the store owner. Hans places his candy on the counter and pays, and then we are back in the street.

"Did you take the egg?" All the play has gone out of my friend.

"Yes," I reply, defiant. "I took it."

"Show me," Hans demands.

We round the corner, and I glance over my shoulder to ensure I am out of the shopkeepers' eyesight. Carefully, I take out the egg.

"You bring it back!" Hans shouts, and I wonder why he sounds so fearful. But Hans' cries are too late; I have already peeled off the foil. I take a bite and offer Hans a piece, but he shakes his head like it's poison. When I reach the chocolate egg's treasure, I crack open the small plastic egg to find the most beautiful necklace I have ever seen, dark blue and sparkly. I proudly put it around my neck and walk down the street with Hans, looking for someone to admire my prize. But Hans will not even look at me.

When we reach home, Mother asks where I got the necklace. I choose my lie carefully.

"Natascha gave it to me."

Natascha is in my class, but Mother does not know her personally, only her name.

"It looks lovely on you, Anne."

I flush with pride. A compliment from Mother—I tell myself that they are so rare that it was worth stealing, although my stomach feels uneasy with the weight of my lie.

A few days later, Hans and I meet in his backyard. This is where we always meet—at the end of our properties where there is no fence, and we can pass from one yard to another. It is the perfect place for hide and seek, which we play with the neighborhood kids. Or we swing on Hans's swing set and hold a competition: who can swing the highest and jump off at the highest point?

At the top of my swing, I see two figures appear in the backyard: Elsa and Gerda.

They are usually not allowed out as they must stay inside and finish their homework. I get a lot more freedom since I am at the top of my class. My sisters must have finished their homework early today.

Though I wish I could have Hans all to myself, I warm to the presence of Elsa and Gerda. The four of us chitchat about friends and school when Hans points to me and blurts out, "Do you know that she has stolen a Kinder Joy egg?"

My sisters look confused.

"Yes," says Hans. "The other day at the bakery." He tells them the whole story, finishing with "that's where she got the necklace."

The necklace becomes a burden around my neck—I want to tear it off and forget I ever saw it. Elsa and Gerda looked at me with furrowed eyebrows. I can't speak; I'm so shocked by Hans' betrayal and paralyzed by my own fear. Before I can find words, Elsa and Gerda turn and fly back toward the house.

"No, don't tell them, please!" I call after them, my heart drumming in my ears. There's no point.

Up the stairs they run and into the house. "Mom, Mom!" I can hear them yelling, even though I am in the backyard, and they are inside. Here is another race between them: who can be the first to find Mom and rat me out.

I turn to face Hans as if in slow motion. Hurt and shock mingle within me. I expect tattling of my sisters—but from Hans?

"I had to tell them," Hans says seriously, sitting on the swing and dangling his feet.

I am trapped but start to run anyway, into the street, blinded by tears. I pass the Drache's house and finally reach the street corner, already out of breath. I think of leaving forever—maybe to the house of one of my parents' friends—but that would be no use. Running there would only buy me a short amount of time; my parents would find me soon enough. I rip the necklace off —I hate it now—and throw it on the sidewalk, then rush around the corner into the next street. Before long, I hear a car approaching. I don't need to look to know who it is.

Mom has found me.

Elsa and Gerda roll down the windows of the car and taunt, "We knew where you were. We just followed the necklace!"

As if I can outrun them, I keep going. Eventually, though, I slow to a walk, my body spent from the run and the sobbing. Mom pulls up next to me.

"Let's talk about this. It is not that big of a deal. Come inside the car."

Seeing no other option, I climb in and sit in silence on the drive home, awaiting my fate.

10 WHEN THE BIRDS STOP SINGING

The next few days are quiet. I don't let myself relax fully. Is it possible that the Kinder Joy egg could be forgotten? That I will escape a terrible punishment?

On Saturday, I receive my answer. Mother looks at me with a frown. "Father wants to talk to you."

I am summoned not to Father's study but to their bedroom. Everything within me sinks: of course, my atrocity has reached Father. Hans told my sisters; my sisters told Mom; and finally, the terrible news has been laid before Father's feet. I have no choice but to accept my fate.

The confidence that had filled me on the day I took the egg has long since been knocked out. On the way to my parents' bedroom, I tremble. Meeting Father here instead of in his study is a very bad sign. Timid and panicked, I knock on the bedroom door.

"Come in."

I like this room and like it not. It smells of older people's stale bed linen combined with Mom's French perfume and Father's fresh aftershave. A huge double casement window front faces the backyard; it is lovely. The glass facade gives sight to a tall old larch; in the cold winters, we sometimes must free its branches from snow to save them from breaking.

Today I can hear the birds sing—blackbirds and throttles—through the open glass door. The light pours into the room. To me it is like a spotlight, illuminating my guilt.

Father stands with his back to me in front of the window facade, his hands behind his back. He is tall, stiff, immobile. Still gazing out of the window he says quietly: "I heard that you have stolen?"

"I heard that you have stolen?"

"Yes."

"Tell me what happened," he continues. His voice is kind and encouraging. I can almost forget the threat it carries.

I tell him everything, but my mind has trouble placing events in the right order. I get muddled, stutter, and ramble on. I am still speaking to Father's back and cannot help but feel very small—like a mouse cowering in a corner before the cat gets ready to make his final attack.

"You know that we don't lie. I have tried to teach it to you over and over again." Father pronounces the words slowly. Finally, he turns to look at me. "Not only is lying is an unacceptable sin, but now you have become a thief."

I nod.

"So, why did you do it?" Father peers at me and shame engulfs me. I see disappointment in his eyes; I have not lived up to his hopes to become like the smart fox.

I try to explain how Hans and I waited in the bakery, how he suddenly grabbed the egg and put it in his pocket, and that he incited me to steal the egg. Yet I cannot find any words to justify my theft.

"But you took the egg, right?" Now Father's voice is sad and quiet, his eyes so mild. He is the kind doctor--the only part of his being I can trust.

It is so hard for me to admit that I stole the egg, that it was my responsibility, that it was wrong. I already regret my stupidity. Perhaps Father will understand. And so, as I retrace the events of that day with Hans, my hopes climb; the mouse comes slowly but steadily out of its corner to face the cat. Maybe everything will be all right.

When Father speaks, my hopes plummet back to earth.

"I have to punish you. You leave me no choice."

My breath catches in my throat as I await my sentence.

"First, I am going to spank you—"

"No!"

I cry out and search Father's face for a sign that he doesn't mean it. Father only closes his eyes and shakes his head, letting me know he will not reconsider his decision. And I know for certain that the mouse is doomed, that the cat will catch it.

Terror grips me. How can he be so cruel? Father has spanked me many times—but he has never announced a spanking, warning me. I recall other spankings, the sting of his hand against my bum. If Father is announcing this ahead of time, how much worse will it be?

Fear invades every cell; I only barely hear the other punishments Father rattles off:

"Confinement for a week . . . bread and water at dinnertime . . . bring the money back to the bakery . . . confess to the pastor on Sunday. I hope that you will never do it again and that you understand stealing is not worth it. I am very upset that you did this to me."

That I did it to *him*. But I had not thought of Father one time when I was in the bakery with Hans. What could Father mean?

Father takes a seat on his brown wooden chair with the

green cushion which sits on his side of the bed. I know what I must do.

I unbutton my pants and pull them down so that my naked skin is visible. The embarrassment makes the anticipation of Father's strike hurt even before I feel it. The birds have stopped singing; in this moment, I want to die. For all that I long to be close to Father, to be before him in this way is too much to bear.

I bend over Father's lap; the smell of his old aftershave and a stale odor from his pants blend in my nostrils. For minutes, there is no sound in the room but the rhythmic slapping of his palm against my bare skin—over and over again. Each new slap brings a stinging pain. A high-pitched sound rings in my ears, and the strain of not crying makes my face feel like it is on fire. I sweat with the effort as his hand leaves red marks on my body and marks on my soul that will stay long after the redness fades. With each strike, I become smaller. Yet I also resent Hans.

Surely at this moment, Hans is playing in the backyard while I am subject to this misery. What punishment will he face? Can't he at least apologize for the betrayal? I want to cry from the unfairness, but I can't show Father any weakness. He hates signs of weakness most of all.

At long last, Father has satisfied his need for punishment. He praises me for my ability to clench my teeth instead of crying. I have at least done this: not cried. I draw myself up, aching, and pull my pants back on. Father doesn't say anything; I understand that I am to go to my room.

On wobbly legs, I somehow make it to my room. No one waits for me at the door.

I have had the punishment of confinement before. For three days at a time, I have been locked in my room for various infractions—lying or disobeying Mom. I have also been served bread and water for dinner while the rest of the family feasted on meat and potatoes and roasted vegetables.

Yet I have never had a punishment so severe: confinement in my room for seven days after school, bread and water for dinner each day. I wonder how I could have fallen so far in a moment of stupid pride. In my bedroom, the fox Father presented to me on the first day of school mocks me with cold, black eyes.

I close the door behind me and fall on the green carpet. The tears finally come, and I cry for a long time.

Of course, no one comes, except to lock the door and walk back downstairs. When my tears stop at last, I take my stuffed animals and arrange them around me in a protective circle. There is Bello, Susi the brown dachshund, Steffi the black poodle, Clarence the lion—named after the lion in my favorite children's television show, Dactari—and Luis the white seal. I sit in the middle of the circle, surrounded by my friends. I take good care of them. At night, these animals share the bed with me so they won't have to be alone on their shelf in the dark. My bed is overcrowded, and I have to maneuver carefully so there will be enough space for me too. But knowing that my animals are comfortable is more important to me than having a lot of room.

I hold Karl, my current favorite animal. He is a soft blue plush half-horse, half-donkey with red eyes made of glass. One of Father's friends gave him to me. Karl's fur is so soft; I love the vibrant blue of it. I squeeze Karl, who smells like comfort, and I dry my cheeks against his softness. At least with my animals, I am not truly alone.

The afternoon stretches before me endlessly. As the sun moves lower in the sky, I play zoo with my animals. When I am done, I pick up a book and read until evening. Eventually, though, I tire of the book and stare out my window into the street. My window overlooks a small cobblestone street; few people pass by. I sigh.

I am learning something in this room: how to be quiet, even invisible. I must concentrate on my sins. It is hard to forget them—the area where Father hit me still burns. I lay on the carpet on my belly. How can I be more obedient next time? How can I be better?

But boredom and loneliness soon distract me from my contemplation. I miss Aunt Anna. She is in a nursing home and cannot rescue me now. All that connects us is loneliness. When my sisters and I visited her on Saturday in her nursing home, she looked so sad when we left. Before Father and Mother decided to put her there, I could see how difficult it was for her to climb the stairs; we'd had to bring her food to the third floor. Then Mom had started yelling when Aunt Anna was not quick enough to use the bathroom. "Can't you use the bathroom on time?" And I saw my dearest aunt sitting on the bed frame looking down like me, ashamed, as mom spit her anger. No longer would I be able to sit in her room reading her stories as she smiled her kind, generous smile.

Then I remember a terrifying thought. Tomorrow I will have to go back to the bakery and admit that I took the egg. What should I tell the manager? Will they allow me back in, knowing that I have abused their trust?

Tomorrow I will have to go back to the bakery and admit that I took the egg. What should I tell the manager? Will they allow me back in, knowing that I have abused their trust?

"Liars and thieves are not to be trusted."

It is a line Father often repeats—and now I have become a thief myself. Elsa and Gerda told me the other day; once thieves have been caught, they are ordered to stay away from stores they have robbed. But if I am banned from Martin's Bakery, my heart really will break in two.

I am distracted yet again—this time by the urge to use the

bathroom. My door is locked; there is no sign that anyone is coming soon. I am not in the mood to call for help.

Instead, I scan my room. I must find a toilet substitute—quickly. I settle on my purple plastic tea can, the one I usually use to play Tea Party. I squat over it and try to aim for the small opening of the can while keeping my balance. When I am finished, I am relieved and ashamed, remembering Aunt Anna and her accident before she was sent away. I hide the can behind my desk so I won't have to see or smell it. Perhaps urinating in a tea can is a skill I will have to become good at during my confinement.

The minutes stretch on. I lay on the carpet on my side with my ear to the floor and try to listen for signs of life in the house, but everything is unnaturally quiet. When I think about how many more minutes, hours, and days I must pass this way....

I cannot; my heart begins beating too fast, and I must focus on something else.

After many long hours, Mother knocks outside my door and undoes the lock. She holds a glass of water and a slice of rye bread.

"Here you go." Mother passes the dinner to me with a frown.

I say nothing and take the plate from her. Silently, I head into the hall and find the bathroom. I use the real toilet, brush my teeth, and scrub my face, which looks tired and sad. I wash all the salty residue from my skin.

Back in my bedroom, I chew the bread and crawl into my bed. I am exhausted by the day's turmoil; soon, I fall into a deep, dreamless sleep.

The next morning, I cannot wait to go to school and get relief from the isolation of my bedroom. But then I remember—I must give the money back to the bakery. Will they punish me as terribly as Father?

I am still sore from Father's beating, can still see the red spots from his hand. There is one silver lining: because of my sin, I am an outcast in the home. Therefore, I do not have to give Father his morning greeting. I am thankful for the small break from him.

At the breakfast table, my sisters and I take our meal in silence. Despite their betrayal, they've helped me a little: they gave me eighty Pfenning, which I am to pay to the bakery for the egg. I will pay Elsa and Gerda back over the next few weeks. Before we leave the house, Gerda says, "Dad told us that we have to make sure you give the money back to Martin's Bakery."

Her expression is critical, like Mom's "As if I could forget?" I wish to say it, but I don't, and neither does Elsa. We head out the door toward school.

Normally, Hans greets me each morning and walks with me to school. But today he is not there; perhaps he has already left or is running late.

I see Hans at school, but we don't talk. I wish I could dissolve the strangeness between us. Have my sisters told him about my punishments? I want to ask him but am too ashamed to bring up the subject.

A new thought: have my sisters or Hans told the other students about my sin? Does the whole school know and see me as a thief?

The thought runs through the back of my mind at recess, when I play Horse with my girlfriends Gabi, Katja, and Bettina: each of us take turns playing the animal, running and bolting through the schoolyard just like Black Beauty. It is there in music class too—my favorite subject. Does Mrs. Schneider know I am a thief? What would she think of me if she did? Surely, she would hate me and no longer put me in the front of the class.

But if Mrs. Schneider knows, she is too preoccupied with preparations for the upcoming class concert to care. We practice our Carl-Orff flute march: dozens of students march on stage in lockstep and follow different synchronized routines. We practice in our uniforms, our turtlenecks, black slacks for the boys and skirts for the girls matching exactly. Tensions are high as we march, and Mrs. Schneider yells a lot today. I know the piece perfectly; my mind drifts to the bakery, what will happen after school.

Finally, school is over. I meet Elsa and Gerda outside of the building and walk with trembling legs to the bakery. My biggest fear is that the owner will yell at me in front of all the other customers. When we arrive at the bakery, I swallow.

"Let me look first to see how many people are in the store."

With timid steps, I enter the store. That wonderful smell—for a moment it soothes me, and then I remember what I must do. There is quite a crowd inside. I step back outside to meet my sisters.

"We can't wait," says Gerda impatiently. "We have to be home at 1 p.m. for lunch. Let's get it over with."

Gerda marches into the store. Seeing no other option, I follow her.

There are four people in front of us. I take the money out of my pocket: eighty Pfennig. Mother gave it to me, but I will have to pay her back. I never could have afforded the egg on my own. Quickly, the coins are coated with my sweat.

Three people in front of us now.

What should I say to the owner? I'd rehearsed a script in my room that morning—but now I can't remember any of it. I consider again telling the story about Hans. . . .

Another person enters and takes his place in the line behind us. The whole story will take too long—I scratch the idea.

Two people ahead of us.

My sisters look around at all of the delicious treats as the line behind us grows longer. With me in the middle, they remind me of two police officers in a bad mood.

Maybe I should just give the owner the money and leave. But what if she asks me what it is for?

My parents have asked me to confess; I know my sisters will report back on whether I have.

One customer in front of us. My heart hammers against my chest. Then, the owner says, "Yes please?"

I stand on my toes so she can see me. "I, uhh, I. . . . "

I plunk the money on the tray. The person behind me shuffles his weight from foot to foot and mutters, letting me know he is in a hurry. I feel his eyes on the back of my head.

"I took an egg the other day," I finally admit.

"What was that?"

"You have to speak up," Elsa scolds.

"I took an egg, and here is the money."

The store owner just stares at me, confused. I point to the Kinder Joy eggs—the source of all my misery—so she will understand.

The owner just stares at me. Is this the moment she yells at me in front of the entire store? Are these my final moments in Martin's Bakery?

But she only shakes her head, takes the money, and calls, "Next, please."

11 JESUS MY FRIEND

Could that really be all? I wait for the owner to realize the severity of my crime and scream at me in front of all the patrons—but the moment never comes. As I leave the store with my sisters, I am both relieved and confused.

Elsa looks at me and shrugs her shoulders. "Lucky you."

At home, my sisters report to Mom that the returning of the money to Martin's was no big deal. "You got away with it, that's all I have to say," sighs Mom.

I have six days left of my confinement with only bread and water for dinner, and the stings from Father's spanking are still sharp. I have not gotten away with anything, and I wonder: how much more humiliation does Mom hope I receive?

As the days of my punishment wear on, Sunday looms before me. That is the day I must confess to the priest. Then I will know once and for all if I am wretched or not—if God views me the same way my parents do.

In the meantime, I stay in my room and think of Hans, who

is surely out playing in the backyard with my sisters as I spend the long afternoon hours alone. I can't help but think that things have changed between us since he told on me to Elsa and Gerda. I fear he is slipping away, falling under my sisters' spell.

At school, Elsa and Gerda are wildly popular. They have the power to enchant groups of children and compel them to do things for them, like carry their backpacks. Father praises my sisters for their easy ability to entertain. I've noticed that on our walks to school, Hans now prefers their company and tries to keep pace with them. He enjoys listening to their stories—being two years older, they know so much more, of teachers and students and the workings of the school. I feel more and more like a third wheel when the four of us are together. The thought of Hans playing with Elsa and Gerda even now, as I am imprisoned with my stuffed animals—the sadness rises in me.

Why did he betray me? Had Hans wanted to prove something to my sisters, that he was a good guy while I was somehow less than the three of them? I *did* feel less—and at the same time, I feel superior to Hans, because I never would have done what he had done. When I am near him now, I am suspicious. I cannot be too careful with my secrets. What has he told his parents about me? I imagine Hans' mother shaking her head: "Be careful about playing with Anne, she may get in trouble again." And if he'd told his parents, surely the whole school knew of my theft too. My teachers and classmates must look at me through the lens of judgment: Anne the thief.

I grow more suspicious of my sisters, also. They must always make themselves the heroes: the good guys who do the right thing, please Mother and Father and speak out against wrong. I would never have ratted out Elsa and Gerda--yet they did it so easily, with pleasure.

At breakfast the next morning, my fears are confirmed: my sisters say they have told Hans about my punishment. I am both relieved that he knows and embarrassed. On the walk to school, Elsa, Gerda, and Hans walk a few paces ahead of me. I linger behind: loneliness takes over again.

The school year is almost over. After third grade, some of my classmates will switch to a school where Latin is introduced in the fourth grade. It is a rigorous school; only the best students will make the switch.

One day in the week of my confinement, Frau Schneider asks the class who will not be back after summer break. Hans' hand shoots up. Open-mouthed, I gape at him. He stares back at me as if to say, "Yes, me. You didn't know?"

I hadn't known; Hans and I have not talked in several days. What else do I not know? A lump forms in my throat; I gag it down.

Even though I am still angry at Hans, I am sad that next year we will not walk to school together. The school Hans will attend, Das Graue Kloster, is competitive and even stricter than ours. How had Hans gotten in? I'd seen his report card; his grades were not as good as mine, and I'd often heard him argue with his mother as she urged him to complete his homework.

Was Hans happy about this? He had friends at our school, and keeping up with the work at Das Graue Kloster would be difficult. It served no use to speculate—the decision had been made.

I have not walked home with Hans since the day he told Elsa and Gerda about the Kinder Joy Egg—he has not waited for me like he used to do—but today I run up to him on the sidewalk.

"So you are leaving?" I ask, out of breath.

Hans answers without looking at me. "Yes, my parents decided."

There seems to be nothing more to say about the matter. We walk home in silence.

As the week of confinement comes to an end, I look to Sunday with both relief and fear. Relief, because it will finally be over; fear, because the pastor will give me God's pronouncement on my character once I confess to him.

Almost every Sunday, my sisters and I make the ten-minute walk to our church, which we call the 'village church' because a long time ago our district of Berlin was a village. We cross an old cemetery and imagine that ghosts are waiting for us on the graves; this Sunday, their presence is especially near. My sisters and I round a corner and the church, built from cobblestones in the 1300s, appears: its small wooden tower is surrounded by oak, chestnut, and acorn trees. Inside the church, only about eighty people fit. On Christmas and Easter, the doors are flung open so worshippers can get enough air; today, there are just a few people. My sisters and I walk alone. Father, not a religious man himself, has required that we receive some sort of religious education as part of our general education. Mother accompanies us sometimes; Father stays home.

I don't mind church. In fact, I like Pastor Rettich, the children's pastor, and the stories he tells us about Jesus and God. Pastor Rettich leads us in engaging conversations and teaches us what we need to know to be good. He is in his sixties, white-haired and with a kind face. When he says the benediction, "Let the children come to me and forbid them not, for such is the kingdom of God," he looks like he means it.

I fortify myself as I walk to the church. Jesus *likes* children; perhaps he will not cast me out because of my sin? Jesus is my last hope. I pray he will still have me.

Throughout the service, I think more of what I will say to

Pastor Rettich than on the content of his sermon. At last, the time draws near: my final punishment. As the service ends, Elsa and Gerda appear at my side to escort me to the pastor.

I know what I must do, and still my mind rebels against it. My sin feels so long ago; must I go through it all again? I'm embarrassed, just as I was in the bakery. After all, Protestants don't confess to the pastor; they keep their sins to themselves and ask God for forgiveness. Father had forced me to engage in a Catholic practice because he likes the Catholic church best. Father thought a confession and ten Ave Marias—or whatever the priest prescribed—would absolve me. But what if I confessed to the pastor, and he didn't know what to do with it?

I stew at Father for placing me in an impossible situation.

I approach Pastor Rettich in the first row of the sanctuary, then wait for the other children surrounding him to be picked up by their parents. Finally, I stand in front of him.

God, please let this be over quickly.

As quickly and calmly as I can, I tell Pastor Rettich about stealing the egg. As he listens, he keeps his eyes locked on mine. He smiles. At last, he speaks.

"Sometimes we do things which are not okay. It is important that you think about this and know you have done something wrong. It is also important that you regret it. Stealing is a sin—you know this—but Jesus forgives us."

With that, Pastor Rettich turns to another child who begs his attention. Could this really be all?

Could this really be all?

I'd expected the pastor to prescribe Ave Marias, to demand that I pray with him right then and there to beg God's forgiveness. Either he got distracted by the child, or Pastor Rettich really didn't think an elaborate repentance ritual was necessary.

I feel tempted to tap his shoulder and ask, "Is that all? Are you sure I don't need to do anything else?" I look to Gerda, who shrugs. Elsa says finally, "Let's go home."

On the way home, it hasn't yet sunk in that my week of punishment is over. I'm not sure if I can accept my freedom.

"He said Jesus will forgive me," I say to my sisters, "but how do I know that?"

"I think you will feel it," Gerda says unconvincingly.

I want to know so much more. What does forgiveness *feel* like? Does it come all at once or little by little? But I doubt my sisters can answer these questions.

We arrive home to the smell of roast, vegetables, and potatoes: Mom's Sunday dinners are not to be outdone. Father asks when I walk through the door: "How did it go at church today? Did you confess to the pastor?"

"Yes."

"And what was his reaction?"

Gerda speaks for me. "She told him everything, and the pastor said that Jesus forgives her."

"That's all?" asks Father.

I note the astonishment in his voice. I wonder, as I had when I told Mom about the bakery owner's reaction to receiving the money, what more had he hoped for?

"Mmm." Father grunts and takes a swig of beer.

That evening, I cannot fall asleep. My mind races with stories of Jesus the pastor has told us, that I have read in my beloved children's Bible. How I love the stories of Jesus welcoming the little children, walking on water, and raising the little dead girl. I find it incredible that Jesus loves children—all of them. According to Pastor Rettich, it was easy for Jesus to forgive me.

I decide that Jesus is invited on all my make-believe adventures. From that moment on, Jesus accompanies me everywhere; he wears his beige robe and holds his shepherd's cane. I imagine him like the pictures in my books, with an oval face and curly long brown hair. He is good-looking, gentle, and soft-spoken. In manner, he is the opposite of Father.

Sometimes, when Jesus goes to talk to God, he gives his cane to me. I love it when this happens because the cane is magic; when I hold it, I have the power to make everyone in my world happy.

Quickly, Jesus becomes my hero and role model. I want to be wise and kind like him. Jesus helps me face the bullies at school; he helps me overcome my deep loneliness. I even change my name in our make-believe games. With Jesus, I am "Jenny," which sounds much cooler than Anne. Jenny and Jesus: the heroes, the popular guys, and the invincible ones. We are always right; nobody can touch us. Jesus forgave me for stealing the chocolate egg. He has a solution to any problem. Nothing is impossible with Jesus at my side; he gives me so much comfort and strength. Even if my sisters or Hans betrays me, if Father beats me, if Hans leaves, and I am left alone yet again—Jesus will never leave.

12 THE WALL

One morning, I am awoken by Mom's shouts calling up the stairs.

"Anne, come downstairs! Breakfast is ready!"

I wipe the sleep from eyes and watch the sunlight falling through my window. It is Saturday, the first day of summer break. I have six delicious weeks of summer vacation stretching before me before fourth grade starts. Today our family is traveling to the Bavarian Forest; it will take six hours to drive there.

I put on shorts and a blue T-shirt with a big colorful flower and rush down the stairs. In the kitchen, I am greeted by the smell of aftershave and coffee: Father.

Father does not normally take his breakfast with the rest of the family—usually, Mom serves him in bed. Yet here he is at the kitchen table, in a short-sleeved shirt and brown linen pants. The sight of him sitting there drinking coffee makes me nervous. I slip into my seat at the table and join Elsa and Gerda, who munch corn flakes, trying to ignore the angry look Father gives me for being late.

Yesterday, Father had announced that we would be leaving

at 8:00 a.m. sharp. He had planned our departure to the minute: my sisters' bedroom was transformed into a packing station, and Mother had supervised as we chose everything we would take for our three-week vacation. Our Mercedes is not big enough to carry more than the necessities for five people, so every item we will take has passed a careful vetting process.

Elsa and Gerda finish their cereal and push back from the table.

"8:00 a.m.," Father reminds them, a threat in his voice.

I am careful not to disturb him, not to even look at him. One wrong word will make Father jump, so I play invisible. I swallow the rest of my cereal and climb the flights of stairs back to my bedroom, where I select which animals will accompany me on our trip. I choose Bello, my fox, and my puppet Fridolin, wishing I could take all of the more than a dozen animals that still rest on my bed.

"Goodbye," I whisper to my remaining friends. I take two books and a deck of cards, which I hope will entertain me for the long drive.

"Show me the passports," Father tells Mother as I reenter the kitchen.

Passports?

Ah yes—I remember that to get to the Bavarian Forest, we must pass through East Germany. I shiver. If we pass through East Germany, we may encounter Russians. Russians control East Germany; they gained control after a big war, and they hold unfair power over Germans. At any moment, they may conquer this part of the city, as well as West Berlin.

I may not always know who my enemies are—they could look like friends in disguise, Elsa, Gerda, or even Hans—yet I know that Russians are not to be trusted. They are the Bad Guys.

Mom places the passports on the breakfast counter.

"Keys?" Demands Father, and Mother presents them. "Picnic?" Mother nods.

"Okay," Father says, checking his watch. "It is 8:00 a.m. Let's go."

I breathe a sigh of relief as Father pulls away from our home, onto the highway. I don't mind that Elsa has forced me to sit in the middle because I am smallest. I am simply happy to have three whole weeks in the Bavarian Forest ahead of me, to get to spend time in the South I have heard so much about. This is where Aunt Anna is from and where Father spent many of his childhood summers.

"Obviously, summer vacations have started," Mom grumbles, looking at the many cars driving in the same direction.

Father accelerates the Mercedes. He drives very fast, but I feel safe in my perch on the middle rear seat. We overtake cars packed with other children; I try to catch their eye and share a smile as we speed down the highway.

We pass through the Grunewald, "Green Forest," and leafy trees engulf us. When we emerge from the trees and back into sunlight, Father slows the car as we approach a service area to our right.

"Look," Mother says. "This is brand new." She points to a round building housing a gas station that reads Dreilinden.

"Yes," Father says. "It opened last year along with the checkpoint. This is the first time in years we can cross the border wall by car and drive through East Germany, but only on the highway." He eyes the line of cars stretching before us. "It appears that many West Berliners are taking advantage of the agreement."

Three policemen in green uniforms appear on the

highway. They signal that we must follow the line of cars into a huge parking lot. Father grunts, maneuvering the car slowly through a row of cones until he finds a spot designated for us by another guard. He dislikes being told what to do. Father checks his watch; when planning our six-hour trip, it appears he did not account for the time a checkpoint stop would take.

"More chicanery," Mother says, shaking her head.

"What's happening?" I whisper in Gerda's ear.

But it's soon plain to see—we're stuck, one of dozens of cars in this sea of people making their transit through East Germany. I look out the window, to a baby crying in the car next to us. Out of the rear window is the Grunewald. On our family hikes and bikes, the forest feels infinite; but one time I had reached an edge, a barbed wire fence. Father had yelled at me to stop immediately. On the other side, he explained, was "No Man's Land."

The name was weird, I thought—but the place must be dangerous, or else Father would not have shouted so loudly. "No Man's Land" meant no one was allowed to go there. I had wondered why but hadn't asked.

I turn to face the front again. I don't see the wall that separates East Germany and West Berlin, only the endless parking lot. The cars are like a pack of horses waiting impatiently behind a starting gate.

"9:30 a.m., and they were not prepared for a crowd," sighs Father. Clearly, the people handling this checkpoint are doing it all wrong.

I pluck a Swiss chocolate from a box in my lap.

Elsa climbs out of the window and sits in the frame, drawing attention to herself as she does so easily.

"See anything?" asks Gerda. They are hoping to spot classmates in the crowd.

"Nope."

Father lights a cigarette, filling the Mercedes with its stink. My sisters and I turn down our noses at the smell.

We move at a snail's pace, inching forward, and I've almost forgotten the carefree hopefulness I woke up with this morning. Finally, we are released from the parking lot and allowed to drive on the highway. Ahead of us is a roofed checkpoint with control boxes in each lane.

"Destination?" Demands the guard in the control box.

"Hof!" shouts Father.

"Safe trip." The guard smiles and waves us through.

"That was quick!" I say, trying to inject cheer into the car.

"Anne, you ninny, this is just the beginning. We have just left West Berlin. This was under the control of the West Allies." Mom shakes her head.

Father clears his throat. "Why do we have the border?" He is no longer the annoyed driver; now his tone is professorial like my teacher, Mr. Coin. He wishes us to know something.

"It has something to do with the war," Gerda replies.

"Yes, which war?" Father turns to face us and smiles.

After we squirm under his gaze for nearly a minute, Elsa finally admits, "We don't know."

Mom glances to Father, then turns to face me and my sisters. "Earlier there was a World War. Many countries fought against each other." Another glance to Father. "This was called the Second World War." We, the Germans, lost the war. The winning countries were called the Allies, and they separated us. We struggled for several years after the war. Many of us starved or died due to the cold winters."

Father has discussed this before. Just the other day, he had forced me to eat detestable, grizzly meat which I had to chew before minutes before swallowing. "You will finish that," Father had said. "You don't know what hunger means."

"The Russians wanted to have their part of our country for themselves, so they built that wall." Mother points to it. "Many

Germans didn't want to live in the Russian East Zone because they didn't want to live with the communists."

Mother spits out the word "communists" like it's a curse word. "They watch everyone, and you cannot openly say what you think." This is her line on the communists, which I have heard often at home.

"Communists" and "Russians"—these are the Bad Guys I have only heard whispers about. To be this close to them chills me. What if the Russians decide to take over all of Germany right now?

"My friend Christa married a pastor. They live in Leipzig," Mother says. "They chose to stay in East Germany. They thought that with God's help, they could manage. After all these years, East Germany still hasn't recovered from the war." She shakes her head.

Our family sent a package to Christa not too long ago, filled with coffee and chocolate. I say a silent prayer for Christa, that she and her family will somehow be all right in the land of the Russians.

We follow the two-lane highway, which leads into a huge curve. I look at the signs which tell us to stay in our lane, and then I see it: a massive black metal roof with white cubicles under it, windows facing the lanes. The cubicles look like our square Lego houses which we built on Sunday mornings while our parents slept; some of the cubicles are filled with men and some are empty. They range in number from one to twelve.

Father maneuvers the car into the eighth queue and shuts off the engine. Men in gray uniforms patrol the line, black guns decorating their backs. The sight brings back a memory I have not had in a long time—my nightmare of the men with uniforms hiding in my room.

I shrink into my seat.

A man with a pale round face appears at our window and knocks. Father rolls down the window.

"The motor must run at all times," the man says grimly. He says it in German, which surprises me—I'd thought perhaps he'd speak Russian.

Father nods and smiles modestly, rolling up the window and turning on the motor. It is strange to see Father take orders from someone else without even a question.

I count eight cars in between us and the first control box.

"And where are the Russians now?" asks Elsa, glancing excitedly from one guard to the next. "Are these guards Russians or Germans? Their German sounds different than ours."

"They are all Germans," Father explains. "They are from Saxony, a federal state in what is now East Germany. This soldier has a strong Saxonian dialect."

I gaze out the window at the men. How can they stand here, checking us? We are Germans too. Perhaps they are forced to do this by the Russians, and that is why they look so grim.

Even though it is scary to be surrounded here by so many East Germans and possibly Russians, I soon grow bored. "When will we be there?" I ask, impatient.

"I don't know how long it will take," Father says, taking out another cigarette and lighting it. He must be furious, his carefully-timed trip bungled by the checkpoint.

My attention is captured by a Volkswagen being searched by a guard.

"What's happening?" Elsa asks, but Mother shushes her, which means she doesn't know.

The car's driver smiles as if she is putting on a brave face, her expression a mix of apology, shame, and suppressed annoyance. But the two kids in the back look terrified. The family is forced out of the car; no one comes to talk to them as a guard pulls the luggage out of the trunk. The family just stands there, helpless, as the guard searches their car—for what? I pity this family. How can people be so mean? How can Germans treat other Germans this way?

Another guard approaches Father's window. "Any weapons in your car? Anything to declare?" he asks in German, his face like a wall.

An unpleasant smell assaults my nose; it comes from the control box and even over-trumps father's cigarette stink. It is a combination of a plastic smell and staleness that contributes to the unfriendliness of this crowded place and spawns a feeling of infinite loneliness.

"What's that smell?" I ask, puzzled.

Mom giggles. "This is the smell of the German Democratic Republic," she says, a hand covering her mouth so the guards will not hear. "It is a disinfectant they use to keep these public places clean."

I cannot tell if this is simply a joke or if there is truth to what Mom says. Does East Germany really smell different from us?

We've reached the cubicle—at last. Father hands over our passports out the window. The man studies them, bored, then scrutinizes Father, Mom, my sisters and I all in turn. He keeps the passports.

"What is he doing with the passports?" I ask, nervous. Will we soon be turned out of our car and searched like the poor family?

"They are running them through a system—see the white pipe?" Father says. While we inch forward, I follow with my eyes the long white pipe which runs to the second cubicle.

"It's 10.15 a.m., and we are still in West Berlin," growls Father. "Let's see how long it takes from here."

I pull cards from my backpack. "Let's play," I say to Elsa, and we play our beloved game, Mau Mau". Elsa has to reach her arm over my lap to put one card on the stack.

"Don't touch my leg."

"Sorry," says Elsa, but then she does it again. Her hand is sweaty, and I am already sweaty enough in the cramped car.

"Don't!" I shout again.

"Girls, stop it," says Mom, turning to scowl at us.

"I don't want to play anymore," skulks Elsa and drops her cards on the floor.

"You have to clean that up," I say, pointing to the cards.

"No, I don't." Elsa leans back in her seat and smirks.

"Stop arguing right now!" yells Mom. She reaches back from her seat, then pinches my calf. Pain sears through my leg.

I wonder how much longer we can stand to stay cramped in this small space when we finally move to the second control station. Same procedure, same smell, same indifferent look from the guards. Look up, look down, look up, look down. Stamp, stamp. At last, the guard tells us: "You can go."

Father follows the cars as the many lines funnel into just two. The forest abruptly ends; there is blank space around us now, to my left and right. No trees, only massive concrete watch towers lined up at short distances with flood lights glaring in all directions. Guards stand atop them with guns. Hungry looking German shepherds pull at metal chains

"This," says Father, "is the death strip."

The name sends another chill through my bones. My sisters and I are silent—no squabbling now. I clutch Bello to my chest and squeeze tight.

Mother and Father discuss how this awful place got its name and I gather that, sometimes, people try to flee from East Germany to West Berlin. Many are shot right here at the death strip. I file this away: Germans shoot at other Germans. How could fellow countrymen hate each other so much?

I am amazed that I never knew such a haunted place existed so close to my home. We drive through the desolate strip until it gives way to the forest once again, and I wonder—was it a dream?

I look behind me to the receding death strip, picture bodies on the ground. Who picks them up? Who informs the families that their son, daughter, father, brother, has been killed in their attempt to escape? Had this been happening while I was safe in my third-floor bedroom, just miles away? What other terrible secrets do Father and Mother keep quiet about?

13 PLAN B

"When will we be there?" I ask Mother and Father as the five of us trudge through a constant drizzle.

We arrived in Bavaria two days ago, after the endless journey through the East Zone. Our destination was Cham, a quaint town in the Bavarian Forest. Father spent most of his summers there as a boy; it's where Aunt Anna lived until she moved into the nursing home. Soon after our arrival, my parents' friend Aunt Siegrid had joined us with her two kids, Katharina and Mathias, whom we call Matze. Aunt Siegrid is not really our aunt, but we call her that to be respectful, just as we call my parents' other grown-up female friends "aunt."

Katharina, Aunt Siegrid, and Mathias are all safe and warm back in the hotel while my family makes this endless trek. It's not fair; I envy them, even though I love Aunt Siegrid. Her husband died two years ago. Since then, she has become especially close with Mother and Father. Aunt Siegrid and Mother are best friends, and Father is godfather to Matze. I wish Mother and Father had chosen to stay at the hotel with them rather than torture us with this endless wet hike.

"Hans?" Father calls to Mother. "Are we close?"

So, Mom doesn't know where we are headed either.

"It should be soon now," grumbles Father.

I am used to this type of excursion, which Father makes us take often. Even though they are difficult, the challenges Father sets for us in the outdoors are a chance to show my toughness, to pretend I am a boy. This long walk reminds me of many Sundays when Father takes us on endless treks through Grunewald Forest, when I careen down steep canyons on my bike on the narrowest paths, the bike flying so fast that I can no longer use the pedals—I ride splay-legged, trying to steady the trembling handlebar. At night, when it is pitch dark, I ride over surface root systems of the old oak and beech trees. I crawl through high grass and creep up to Father. Or I swim across the Havel River, populated by steamers and boats, following Father's head as it pushes forward in the agitated water. Although I think I will drown, I do not cry; in my head, I even make fun of girls who *do* cry. I will not show weakness. I will make Father proud. I wish I could be a boy—I see that in every way, their lives are better. Teachers prefer boys; I see how Father talks to Matze in an intimate, manly way which he never uses with us, his daughters.

Today, my clothes are soaked. The wind has picked up; I pull my too-thin anorak tighter around me. Father and Elsa walk ahead of Gerda and Mother, and I bring up the rear. I look at their figures, bent over against the weather.

Normally, Father knows the correct routes for our hikes; today, I suspect he is guessing at something. We detour around some smelly granges, follow the lane straight up the hill. At last, a secluded house comes into sight—then a castle tower on top of the hill. The drizzle turns into a downpour.

The five of us run up the hill towards the castle, Mom cradling her head in her arms in vain, trying to protect her meticulously teased hair. From the top of the hill, we can see a village; it appears as if time has stood still here for the last one hundred years. The village houses stretch down the hill, and a cobblestone street runs through the small town. We follow the cobblestone street past the small houses, which don't even have light in the windows. The small street turns onto a bigger one, and we pass an abandoned phone booth standing near a traditional Bavarian maypole, two grain wreaths and a soaked Bavarian flag hanging heavy from the top. Behind the maypole is a hog house where pigs drowse in the mud and fill the air with the scent of old dung.

Where on earth are we going?

"The house must be nearby," says Father as though as he has read my mind, scanning the landscape. We follow him onto a lot with an open gate. "This could be it. Wait."

What house?

But Father does not explain: he is a man of few words and does not share the plans in his head. Father leaves and goes —where?

Mom begins to explore the lot, and my sisters and I follow. We've arrived at a shabby old house, and the rain has picked up again, pouring as it can only pour in the Bavarian Forest—a rain which never seems to stop, which turns everything gray and makes me think the world will drown. The rain makes the house look especially uninviting.

I study the structure made of white stone and wood, with a dark roof. The house resembles a Bavarian farmhouse: in the olden days, the farmers had lived on the second floor and kept stables on the lower floor. I dislike the small windows, which were made that way on purpose to keep the cold out. A balcony runs along the backyard side, and wooden beams are strewn about the yard. It is clear the place has not been kept up in some time: the wide grass land in the back has turned into a swamp.

At long last, Father returns with an old man whom he introduces as Hans Dietl. Hans Dietl is almost completely bald;

his round glasses give him an intellectual air. When Mr. Dietl speaks, his Bavarian accent is so thick I can't understand a word. Father has to translate. He explains:

"The owner of this place has gone bankrupt due to gambling debts. On the day the executor came to the property with Hans Dietl, the owner had stood in front of the house with a rifle, blocking the entrance. But thanks to Mr. Dietl's intermediary skill, the man had finally given in."

It is an interesting story, but I have no clue what it has to do with us. Also, I feel sorry for the man. Had his family lived here for decades? Where are they now?

Mom furrows her eyebrows. "Hans, I didn't know this place was in such poor condition." We should have looked at it before you bought it auction. I mean, look at this dirt! This chaos!" She looks down at her boots which have sunken in the mud, disgusted.

My brain tries to comprehend what Mom just said: *Father owns this house?*

"It will do," Father replies, confident. "Now we have a house to go to in case West Berlin becomes occupied by the Russians. Here in the countryside, we will be safe. No one will bother us." Father grows more animated as he speaks. "And we will get real passports, not the auxiliary ones we have now as West Berliners."

He turns to my sisters and me now, lecturing. "As you know, not only is Germany divided—so is Berlin. The wall divides us, West and East. West Berlin is surrounded by the Russians. We are a small island—free—but not really a part of West Germany. The Allies left it this way." The contempt in his voice is unmistakable.

He continues, "Christiane, you remember when the Soviets boycotted West Berlin, and General Clay, the American General, gave the order for the Berlin airlift?"

"Yes, I remember! That was such a scary time! I was only thirteen, but I remember the headlines in the newspapers."

"Well, that was in 1948 and lasted almost a year. General Clay had the courage to set up an incredible feat of logistics when cargo planes landed every four minutes, twenty-four hours a day. He saved so many people from starving, and finally, the Soviets gave in. I don't want to experience this threat again."

I picture our family on an island surrounded by Russians who lean by the thousands over the wall, pointing their guns straight at us. I shiver.

Mother asks, "But Hans, is this necessary—"

Father cuts her off with a raised hand. There is a growing intensity in his eyes, a look I know to fear.

"I've seen The Great Depression and a World War, only twenty-one years after the first Great War that killed my father. With the Russians on the other side of the wall, we cannot simply put our heads in the sand and pretend Berlin is safe. The auxiliary passport reminds us we are not safe. We need a plan B." Father strides about the yard. "This place is simple, yes, but it is all we need. I've bought a potato field too. If there is another food crisis as we had when the Russians locked up West Berlin, we can survive. We can grow our own food."

Images flash through my mind: the guards at the border with black rifles on their backs. Bombs dropping on Berlin. Mother and Father in a field, hastily gathering potatoes before running back to the safe house: *this* house. Our home.

Fear claws at my gut. All my life, I have heard of the danger posed by the Russians. The Russians are an ever-present threat, the boogeymen that come in the night. Yet despite the danger they threaten, my family has carried on as normal. Until now.

Father has taken the drastic step of buying a safe house, hours away from Berlin, sight unseen. What can this mean but that the threat is getting closer? How much longer until the

Russians invade and life as I know it ceases to exist? Will we make it out in time? What of my friends in Berlin, who have no safe houses? Will the Russians show them mercy?

Danger feels closer than it's ever been. Close as the men in my room from my childhood nightmare, gray-uniformed and holding rifles by my bedside.

Father enters the house after Hans Dietl. My mother, sisters, and I follow them.

"Be careful!" says Father, climbing a narrow dark staircase. "Hans mentioned that the floors might have a hole here and there. So, watch your steps."

Inside, the house smells mold and old wood. There is an outhouse, stuck onto the main house and hidden behind a large bush.

Mom cannot stop shaking her head. I can almost feel her longing—for our large, beautiful home in Berlin, our housekeeper, our well-kept yard.

Later, my sisters and I explore the backyard. Behind two tall fir bushes is the wreckage of a swimming pool, with cracks on the sides and a puddle of black water in its center. I crinkle my nose at the rotten smell and shiver, soaked through from our hours in the rain. Water from my anorak hood splashes onto my face. Again, I think of Aunt Siegrid, Matze, and Katharina back in Cham and dry at the hotel.

Finally, Mr. Dietl extracts his car from the backyard swamp and drives us back to Cham. On the drive, he teaches us how to pronounce the name of the village: "Sattelpeinstein."

Several weeks later, back in Berlin, Mother shows me her new passport. Father has made good on his promise to get us real ones. There is my name on Mother's passport, listed under "children." But I am surprised when I see what Mother has listed as her primary place of residence: Sattelpeinstein. Now we are citizens of West Germany.

PART 2

14 MEN IN MY ROOM II

I am nine when the men appear in my room again.

They appear on the island of Sylt, off Germany's northern coast in the North Sea. I go there to Aunt Siegrid's cottage sometimes, when Father and Mother take trips with my sisters or on their own. Like Sattelpeilnstein, I call it home. There I learn to ride a horse and enjoy bathing in the cold sea. I like the windy weather and our long hikes in the shallows.

This time, Father has come with me. We rode side by side on the train to Hamburg and then on the small propeller aircraft to Sylt. I sat by him on the short plane ride, unsure of how to act with him right next to me, on this trip I usually take with Aunt Siegrid and her children. But Father became preoccupied with a medical lecture, and soon I could relax.

On this island, Father is kinder to me. I wonder if it is because he is with Aunt Siegrid; he is always in a better mood when she is around. Aunt Siegrid is pretty—curly auburn hair, a stylish widow in her forties. She is over at our house so often she is like a second mom. I enjoy when she visits us; it means Father is distracted and picks on his daughters less. He, Aunt

Siegrid, and Mom stay up late into the evening when we children are asleep. Aunt Siegrid reminds me of a lion tamer in a cage with two predators: Mother and Father.

Father and I stay in a hotel this trip; it is here that the men in gray soldiers' uniforms reappear in my room at night. I wake up, bathed in sweat.

"Father," I cry out. There is no reply. Where can he be?

I can't stay here; I am too frightened. I rush out of the room, so distracted that I bump into an old lady.

"What is it, child? Are you lost?"

I have been trained not to speak to strangers. But the dream is too real, the fear too great.

"I am—I am looking for my father," I sputter. "I'm not sure where he is."

"Well, I cannot help you with that," says the lady; then she walks away. I am angry at myself for talking to her—no good comes from talking to strange people. I sit on the staircase that leads to the entrance hall and wait for Father, wrap my arms around my body, and shiver. Although it is strange to sit out in the open like this, I know I am safer here, among hotel guests, than back in the room with the men.

At last, I see Father coming into the hotel lobby, buoyant. A few women stand at the counter and wait for their keys; they turn to look at him with glowing eyes. Then, I understand something new: women *like* Father. They look at him with admiration. Father has a presence; he fills up a room with his charm. Amid the fond looks of the women, Father looks ten years younger. He greets them with sparkling eyes.

Then Father spots me. "What happened? Why did you leave the hotel room?"

His voice, kind and out of breath, puzzles me. In his eyes, I recognize the mildness reserved for when I am sick. He sounds so caring, and it is so unexpected I begin crying. How desperately I want not to cry in front of Father—but I am so relieved he is not angry, I lose my composure.

It is so difficult to cry in front of Father because I try to do it just right. Father has said that girls should always cry beautifully, not screaming and whining like crybabies. At all times, girls must remain pretty. And so I try to appear pretty, but I cannot control my facial features. My eyes burn like fire, but I resist rubbing them and let the tears stream down my face—gracefully. I look at Father and try to smile.

"I . . . I had this nightmare again."

"What nightmare?" Father asks softly.

I swallow. "That there were men in the hotel room in uniforms. They chased me. They wanted to kill me."

I wait for Father to calm my fears, tell me that what I saw was nothing. But instead, he looks as if he's seen a ghost.

"In uniforms? What kind of uniforms?"

"Gray uniforms," I answer slowly. "They had gray caps, too. And guns."

Father shakes his head, his expression one of disbelief.

"Could it be that . . . it reminds me of. . . ."

Father leads me back to the hotel room, murmuring and shaking his head. *Reminds you of what?* My mind screams—but I don't press, and Father doesn't expand. We go straight to bed.

That night, Father snores, and I can barely sleep. Father seems to think the men are real, to recognize them from some place. I am both comforted and frightened by this—because if the men are real, what's to stop them from visiting tonight? It has been some time since their last appearance, yet they feel closer than ever. It's as if they have a message for me—something I must know. The message grows closer.

Yet the next morning, Father is in the bathroom, whistling a tune which he practices on violin every evening—a happy, uplifting song. It is hard to remember the terror of the night before with Father in such a jaunty mood. Still, fear lingers around the edges of the hotel room.

In the coming months, weeks, days, it will stalk closer and closer.

And closer.

15 TREBLINKA

One Saturday afternoon in winter, Mother announces to Elsa, Gerda, and me: "Michelle will be coming tomorrow afternoon. He needs company. I hope we can cheer him up a bit."

I have seen Michelle Schwalbe before at Father's music evenings. He is the concert master of the Philharmonic Orchestra. Michelle is a small man and wears thick, black-rimmed glasses, his black curly hair always neatly combed back. He is severe and moody and scares me a little. I am not surprised at Mom's saying Michelle needs "cheering up"—he always seems grumpy—but I wonder how we are supposed to help. I feel shy in his presence; people fawn over Michelle because of his skill at playing the violin. When he plays Mendelssohn or Brahms or Schubert with Father and his friends, people flock to listen.

Perhaps Michelle makes me nervous because he makes *Father* nervous. With Michelle, Father plays second violin. Michelle is exacting; he often interrupts and wants to repeat certain passages until they are exactly right. Father wants to just get through the music; I can tell that something about Michelle annoys him.

My sisters and I gather in the living room for "Kaffee und Kuchen" —coffee and cake— a traditional German afternoon treat. Mother has purchased the delicious Wiener Konditorei cake from the Roseneck bakery. She does not go to such lengths for just anyone.

When he arrives, Michelle wears a black coat and white silk shawl. He has come without his violin today—strange. Michelle's cologne smells fresh, Oriental, and expensive. When he speaks, his voice is high-pitched and raspy, and he throws in many French words. I have a hard time understanding him.

Michelle speaks animatedly with Father about his work with the Philharmonic, the rehearsals, Mr. Karajan, the Philarmonic's dynamic and infamous director. "Hans," he asks my Father, "should I start a solo career, or is it too late? What would Karajan say if I left?"

I sit carefully on the sofa, unsure of how to act in the face of Michelle's distress. It is unusual for my sisters and me to be included in a gathering of my parents' friends. Michelle is clearly bothered—he seems almost haunted. He speaks as if he has lost all confidence in his ability to play. But something more gnaws at him, something beyond his position at the Philharmonic. When Father tries to offer advice, Michelle keeps talking, restless.

I can sense that Father is getting upset, and I mentally beg Michelle to stop. It is the way Father toys with his fork and lets his eyes wander that alerts me to danger. But then I remember that Michelle has nothing to fear from Father's wrath; it is only his daughters and wife who must tread carefully.

At last, Father gets up; he has an important phone call from the hospital.

Michelle ceases his tirade and follows Father's retreating figure with tired eyes. I glance outside to the trees in our backyard, longing to make an escape of my own—but there isn't one. The sun sets slowly; the approaching darkness is like a drop of black ink spreading through a beaker of water, darkening it. Michelle sits opposite me, peering at nothing through his black-rimmed glasses, his chocolate cake untouched.

Suddenly, he sits upright. "Christiane, do the kids know what happened to me?"

I glance to Mom, whose eyes go wide for a fraction of a moment. She shakes her head and smiles politely.

"You know," says Michelle, "I was thirteen years old when I graduated from high school in Warsaw." He leans over the coffee table; his eyes take on a new glint, dark and dangerous. "I had the gift of playing the violin and always dreamed of a solo career. Soon, I moved to Paris and continued my studies. Until the Nazis invaded."

Nazis? It is a word I have heard before but cannot assign to a meaning.

"In 1940 I was able to flee to Lyon and got an engagement with the Symphonie Orchestra. Lyon at that time was not part of the Vichy Regime. I was able to stay with them until 1944, but then I had to flee again. This time in a furniture van."

Is he making it up? I feel Mom's tenseness. Just the other day, Mom had complained about how much Michelle talks. She said we shouldn't take what he says at face value.

My mind sticks on *Vichy Regime*—another phrase I have never heard before. I glance to Elsa and Gerda, whose faces have almost disappeared in the wintery dusk. It seems that Michelle's voice has made the night fall more quickly.

I glance to Michelle, who appears lost in his memories. All signs of restlessness are gone. Mom gets up to go into the kitchen, and my sisters and I are left alone with this haunted man.

"Why did you have to get out of Paris?" Gerda asks.

"I am a Jew. And the Nazis were prosecuting us. Don't you know about this?"

I don't understand what Michelle is saying—should I know? Elsa and Gerda squirm on the sofa and avoid Michelle's gaze. They look as if they know something about what Michelle is saying. What could he mean? I heard the word "Jew" before. Is it someone from another country? From his accent, I thought Michelle was French or Polish.

But from my Bible stories, I have learned that Jesus was a Jew who was killed. Now I am a Christian because of Jesus. I think of asking Michelle what all that means, but I don't dare. His eyes are too intense.

He continues,

"The furniture van brought me to Switzerland at the end of the war. I was only twenty-five by then. I met Furtwängler and Toscanini. I played as concert master in the Orchestra de la Suisse Romande."

Michelle stands and paces around the table, agitated. He comes to a halt behind a chair, inches from me and my sisters. He speaks on with his raspy voice; I try to follow the story, but it is difficult because of Michelle's many French words and the place names and phrases he uses, which mean nothing to me. Yet Michelle speaks with such intensity; there is something he is desperate that we know.

"The violin saved my life. But it didn't save Mutti's nor my sister's life. I tried to get them out! But it was too late." I am both shocked and scared to see tears run down his face; I have to lean forward to hear him better.

"What happened to them?" Gerda wants to know. There is dim understanding in her eyes; she knows more about what Michelle is saying than I do.

Mom reenters the room with more tea. I look to her face and see understanding there. She knows the story.

She puts the tea on the table and leaves the room again. Why doesn't Mother stay with us?

"My mom and sister died in Treblinka. I am the only one who survived from my family."

Treblinka. He says the word so matter-of-factly, with such sadness, as if everyone in the world knows about it. Michelle looks again to my sisters and me, and I can feel his sadness and I wonder what I can do to make his sadness go away.

He continues, "Do you know how many of us the Nazis killed?"

We shake our heads, tentative.

"Six million. Can you believe it, six million!"

The number flies from his mouth and hits me between the eyes; my sisters and I move on the couch, uncomfortable and frightened. Michelle is no longer dejected. Now I can see his eyes filled with rage.

Still, his words make no sense to me. I am ten years old, but I feel grown up now after hearing Michelle's story and being treated as an adult. I wonder how something so unthinkable could happen—six *million* people. It was not such a long time ago. Father has spoken of the Nazis. He has mentioned the good things he learned from them—to show courage, for example. Father, who always reads newspapers and loves history—surely he could not have left out this detail, this unimaginable number. *Six million.*

Mom has spoken about the war, yet she has never mentioned Jews being killed. Neither has Omi Dina, who has shared so many fascinating, conflicting stories about her war experiences. She ones mentioned that their publishing house in Göttingen suffered under severe censorship during the Third Reich and that they had worried that Opi could be arrested by the Nazis or could have been sent to war. But she also proudly mentioned that she had received the "Cross of Honor for the

German mother" from Hitler because she gave birth to five children.

My mind erects a barrier; on one side is what Michelle says. *The Nazis killed six million Jews, including my mother and sister.* On the other side are the stories I have learned from Father and Mother and Omi. Both things cannot be true; so, for the moment, I choose to believe my family's stories.

And yet there is Michelle, his eyes pleading with my sisters and me.

"*You.*" The weight of the word drops like an anchor into the sea. "You have to make sure this never happens again."

Then, I am reminded of a black and white picture I saw long ago: two men hanged from a tree. One wore a sign around his neck that read simply: Jew.

My religion teacher had shown it to me—when? I could not place the picture into any context at the time, so it is hard for me to remember now.

I force myself to meet Michelle's eyes. He leaves soon after; perhaps he has relieved himself of a fraction of his invisible burden.

His scent hangs in the room long after he is gone.

16 REMEMBER ME

The memory of Michelle's visit never leaves me. Two years after that strange afternoon, my seventh-grade class takes a field trip to the Jewish Center. The Jewish Center is in the realm of the Kurfürstendamm, the center of West Berlin. I do not know what to expect from the field trip, but I can tell it will not be lighthearted and fun, like our trips to zoo, ethnological museum, or aquarium, because the adults around us all wear somber faces.

We are met at the entrance to the Jewish Center by another man with a grave face. He leads my class into a spacious hall, where brown metal folding chairs have been erected and face a big TV screen. The room is clean, serious. There are no windows, only black and white photographs that sparsely decorate the white walls.

My classmates mirror the adults around us; no one dares joke or cut up. We are careful not to speak to one another. The solemn guide clears his throat.

"A synagogue was once on this ground," he explains. He talks about its former grandness: a neo-Romanesque structure with Byzantine elements, completed in 1912 as a symbol of

Jewish emancipation in the German Empire. It could accommodate nearly 2,000 worshippers, but it was destroyed on November 9, 1938 by the Nazis.

Nazis. I shudder. Our guide speaks their name not as Father—with a kind of fondness—but as Michelle had, as if he can barely bring himself to utter the word.

A side door opens; an older man, bent with age, enters. His hair is silver gray, and his face is lined with wrinkles. He wears a suit too big; the man's thin frame swims in it. Had I passed this man in the street, I wouldn't have looked twice.

"David Rosenstein is going to tell us his story now," says the guide. The man gives a little bow.

"I am a survivor of Nazi Germany," begins David Rosenstein. His voice is so soft I have to bend forward to listen. He speaks of what it was like as the Nazis gained power, the fear that his parents and siblings felt. Mr. Rosenstein's parents did whatever they could do to get him out of Germany, sending him to London—if he says how they knew to do this, or why they didn't send his other siblings too, I am unable to hear. Mr. Rosenstein tells us that shortly after he left for London, his parents and siblings—Esther and Aaron—were transported to Auschwitz. "I never saw them again."

I recall Michelle's haunted look over coffee and cakes in the living room. Here is another man who lost his whole family. If Mom, Father, Elsa and Gerda were suddenly gone, and only I was left, what would I become?

Michelle calls our home almost every day now. The torment he felt on the day he told us of Treblinka seems to have grown. Mother can tell by the ring of the phone that it is him, as he calls around the same time each day. She is patient and listens to his monologues, of how he is so lonely in his apartment and needs to talk to someone. I notice that even though he is *Father's* friend, not Mother's, Father always finds an excuse not to talk to Michelle. At least Michelle has the violin to soothe his heartache.

What does Mr. Rosenstein have?

Mr. Rosenstein has stopped talking. A heavy silence falls around the room. Our guide is the one who breaks it.

"Before 1933, the Jewish community in Berlin counted 160,000 members. In 1945, only 8,000 were left." He glanced around the room. "Does anyone have a question?"

Michelle had said that six *million* Jews were killed. 160,000 was a tiny fraction of the whole, but only 8,000 left meant that around 150,000 died or were displaced.

Discretely, I turn my gaze to Rebecca, Ariana, and Josh, the Jewish students in our class. Obviously, their families were brave enough to come back. They stare at the guide without moving. No one raises a hand.

No one raises a hand.

The guide continues. "I am going to show you a documentary about the Holocaust."

I have heard the word "Holocaust" before; earlier that year, a miniseries with the same title had run on German televisions at nine in the evening. "I forbid you to watch it," Father had said. "It is American propaganda, and it is too late for you anyways." But most of my classmates had seen it. The show caused a huge outcry in West Berlin—over what I wasn't sure, since talk of the miniseries was strictly forbidden in our home. Whenever the subject came up with guests at one of Father's dinner parties, Father changed the subject.

I cannot help but feel as if I am breaking a sacred rule as the guide turns on the television, and my eyes remain glued to the screen.

As the documentary unfolds, I cannot believe what I see. The show opens with dead bodies in shredded clothes lying on barren, treeless ground. The camera pans out; more corpses come into sight. How many—fifty? No, much more—one hundred, or hundreds—maybe thousands. Some of the naked corpses are recognizable as women and children. I swallow bile rising in my throat.

The voiceover in the documentary explains that German soldiers who had been arrested by the British allies had to dispose of the bodies by hand. I watch in horror as the Germans casually, carelessly carry the corpses, which must be featherweight, and dump them into a mass grave. The Germans haul them over their shoulders, pluck them from a truck packed with bodies, drag them along the ground by a foot. A guard gives a shove; a body tumbles to its final resting place, where it is one of thousands. No signs of remorse or shame appear on the German guards' faces. The sight is too terrible to believe.

The voiceover explains that this footage is from a liberated concentration camp. *Treblinka, Auschwitz*—these must be concentration camps too. The voiceover continues; sanitary conditions were so terrible that eventually, heavy machinery was required to move the bodies. I watch in shock as a bulldozer shovels corpses from the ground to the pit. Because there are so many bodies, the bulldozer's shovel is not able to get everyone—some slide to the ground helplessly and remain behind as others are dumped into the grave. These corpses must be pushed; they fall like marionettes, their arms and legs dangling and flailing like sticks. Their mouths are frozen open in a final scream of terror.

How many Esthers, how many Aarons lay in this pit?

I sit there helplessly as waves of horror roll over me. If I could not believe what Michelle was saying—*six million people*—now I cannot deny it. The picture is before me in black and white.

What had I been doing on the nights the miniseries aired and the people of West Berlin watched in shock? Perhaps I was in my room, mooning over or a boy, or doing stupid homework.

I cringe. I cannot believe this knowledge has been kept from me, that I have been going about, stupid, unaware of what happened in this country just thirty years ago.

Now the camera zooms to a barrack where men lie on three-story shelves, lined up like cattle. They gaze exhausted into the camera. The men look barely alive—some grin at their liberators, the British allies, with mouths that have no teeth. Their eyes are like holes in their faces. Now the video shows some men too weak to walk; they must be carried by the British. Some people just stand rooted to the spot—draped in blankets, vacantly staring into the distance. I wonder what they are thinking. Maybe they are happy to be alive; maybe they are thinking about the impossibility of carrying on after all they have seen and lived through.

At last, the documentary ends; the guide flips off the television. "Does anyone have a question?"

I have millions of questions, but I cannot form words.

"We must make sure this atrocity never happens again," he says, and I hear Michelle say, "You must make sure this never happens again."

You.

If I ever have a child, I will give them a Jewish name. I will honor the lost siblings and fathers and mothers and grandparents and cousins in that pit. Whatever else happens in my life, I will not forget.

At the same time, I am confused. How could this happen? Surely if Jewish people were in danger again, everyone would step up and defend them. Omi Dina had sent me a book for my thirteenth birthday about the Scholl siblings, students, and members of the German Resistance who were executed by the Nazis. If the Nazis gained power again, I would join the Resistance like Sophie Scholl. Did Father know about Sophie Scholl?

Father—I thought of what he would say about the

miniseries. He would say it was exaggerated; the Holocaust was over, and reparation fees had been paid. This is what he says when the subject comes up, although I don't know what "reparation fees" are. But how could any amount of money make up for all those brothers and sisters and mothers and fathers in the pit?

Out of my class of twenty-eight, no one speaks as we leave the Jewish Center. I am desperate to share my thoughts with someone, yet I have no idea how. I feel completely powerless, with nowhere to place the terrible knowledge I have just gained.

Yet I must talk to someone.

"How was school today?" Father asks that night at the kitchen table.

"We went to the Jewish Cent—"

Gerda cuts me off with a kick under the kitchen table. Father shoots me a withering look, almost as if he is daring me to go on. I summon my courage.

"We went to the Jewish Center. Ahh, a man, umm, told us about the time under the Third Reich."

Mother gets up, saying something about needing salt from the pantry. I'm reminded of how she kept leaving when Michelle told us about Treblinka.

I gaze around the table, wondering if anyone will pick up the conversation thread where I've left it. Elsa? Gerda? Who can tell me more, help me make sense of the terrible things I saw this morning on the television?

Everyone stares at their plates chewing on their sandwiches. Finally, Father breaks the silence.

"You know, we didn't know what was happening." Who is *we*? Father continues, "Nobody knew, and besides I was fighting in the war. I was part of the Wehrmacht."

I know this: that Father was part of the Third Reich's armed forces.

Father takes a swig of his beer. "In the Great Depression, bread cost one Reichsmark one day and 1000 Reichsmark the next. I saw people carry laundry baskets full of money around, just to buy milk."

I had found some old Reichsmark once, in the laundry room. They were worthless—you couldn't even buy chewing gum with them. Father said he kept them always, to remember the 20's and the Depression.

What does this have to do with the Holocaust? I want to ask, but I don't. Father goes on.

"I saw many men during this time. They would stand around soccer fields and smoke cigarettes. They had nothing to do, no way to feed their families." Father's voice grows even deeper. "You cannot imagine how desperate these people were. And then overnight, everyone had found a job. It was like a miracle. There was food on the table again. Hitler gave these men their honor back."

But we are not talking about Hitler. Tell me about the murdered Jewish people.

"Under Hitler, it took only two hours by train to get from Hamburg to Berlin." Father's voice booms. "This had never happened before. And he built the Autobahn too."

I glance to Elsa, who rolls her eyes at me. Father has made this speech before.

"But what about the benches in the park, the ones that said Not for Jews? Didn't you see them?" I ask the question even though my voice shakes.

On November 9, 1938, in Kristallnacht, Jewish stores were raided, and Jews were run into the streets and humiliated, beaten, and killed. Father had been twenty-three. He'd studied near Nuremberg in Erlangen. He *must* have seen the synagogues burn.

I think also of the book burning of Germany's most famous authors, which had been led by Germany university students. "Aktion wider den undeutschen Geist," they called it: "Action against the anti-German mind." Had Father taken part?

Father acts as if he did not hear my question about the park benches. "I only learned about the Jewish camps after the war. I had no idea what was happening."

I note the defensive edge in his voice.

Yet even as I try to square Father's denials against the truth of what I've seen in the Holocaust documentary, things don't add up. Father has always been interested in politics, has always chosen to read the newspaper and history books instead of novels. He's never said an ill word to say about Hitler. But Hitler had said the Jewish people would be Germany's ruin and described them as vermin, needing to be eliminated. How could Father claim innocence?

Father speaks about how he was eager to join the war effort after he became a doctor, then became an officer in the Wehrmacht soon after joining. He speaks of parades in Nuremberg, how Hitler marched triumphantly through the streets, how he gave people hope, and how the men assembled told Father it felt as if Hitler looked only at them. I recall the pictures I have seen in one of my schoolbooks: ghastly nightly parades, thousands of searchlights funneling meters high into a tea-colored sky. I imagine that in the background, Wagner music plays: maybe the overture to Die Walküre or Götterdämmerung. I see the showmanship and spectacle of it all.

"He was like a father figure to so many." Again, Father takes a swig of beer. The way he speaks, it is as if he watched the war unfold on a movie screen—not as if he was an active participant. But how could he not have been?

"I felt guilty when I had to leave my comrades behind at the front and was sent home. I wanted to stay with them. But Hitler wanted me to come back home because I was the only one in our family who carried the name Witzgall. That's why I survived. I was deployed in Belgium first, then in France. But the real war started in Russia. I have seen dead soldiers with cut out eyes. So many died in Russia," he continues, and I can see his thoughts wander while he stares holes into the door behind me.

Mom clears her throat. "During the war, we had two sheep, Berta and Mathilda." She wears a forced smile. I know what she is doing—trying to change the conversation to something less fraught.

"Christiane, another beer." Father holds up his glass, his voice rough.

I've heard the story of the sheep, and I like it. "Let me get it," I say so Mom can continue.

"I said Christiane," Father answers, and Mother gets up and serves him obediently. He grimaces. "Christiane, you never experienced the hardships I had to endure. Your parents always were wealthy enough to get through the hard times at the end and after the war."

I wonder why he is so resentful of Mother's upbringing. I see how Mother swallows his accusation, looking helpless, unsure how to counter his argument when he is already continuing: "Can't they talk about another subject in history class? How many times did you learn about it?" He points to Elsa and Gerda.

"Every other year," answer my sisters.

"You should learn about more important topics," Father grumbles, getting up from the table and retreating to his study.

I think about the hundreds of bodies in the pit, the haunted faces of the men stacked in barracks. I think of Michelle and Mr. Rosenstein, their entire families gone.

What could be more important?

17 THE NEW TRUTH

A few days after our visit to the Jewish Center, Mr. Schwertfeger, our history teacher who always wears the same yellow slipover, writes "Antisemitism" on the chalkboard.

"Now class," he begins. "Who can tell me what this word means?"

Mr. Schwertfeger carefully guides the discussion that follows. Ariana and Rebecca, twin sisters who are Jewish, talk animatedly. They speak of their many friends who lost family members during the Nazis' rule. Ariana's and Rebecca's grandparents were eliminated. Josh, another Jewish boy in class, had an uncle, aunts, and grandparents who were killed. The conversation is led by these three and Johanna, their friend. No one else dares say anything as my four classmates recount their stories of loss.

As they speak, confusion roils through my brain. Surely there must be some element of the story everyone is missing. I think of Father, his story of how German men went from unemployed and desperate to providing for their families overnight. How does this narrative fit into the story that Ariana, Rebecca, Josh, and Johanna share?

Clearly, Father has only told my sisters and me a different version of history in his stories about the war. And here are my classmates recounting a much more disturbing story. Is there a bridge that connects the two stories—some crucial misunderstanding that everyone has overlooked?

I must know. Tentatively, I raise my hand and hear my heart beating. When Mr. Schwertfeger calls on me, my voice shakes as I speak.

"Hitler got rid of unemployment, and he also built the Autobahn."

The classroom is silent, as if everyone waits for me to finish my thought—but that is the end of it. Yet buried deep within me is the question I cannot speak aloud, the question I don't even know how to form myself. *Tell me why Father has been quiet about it for so long?*

Then I realize something; no one has said the name "Hitler" aloud. My classmates' reaction to my utterance of the "H" word is the same as if I had said "shit" or "fuck." At the Jewish Center, our guide had referred to the Nazis, Germany, and the Third Reich. I wish someone would say one of those words, if only to lessen the sinking sensation taking over my gut—the feeling that I have made a horrible mistake.

"You Nazi."

It is Ariana who breaks the silence. Her words, spoken with a hoarse, strained voice, come from behind me and hit the back of my head hard as if she had thrown a rock.

"That is exactly why Hitler was so successful," Ariana continues. "He used the Autobahn to get the troops to war. He solved unemployment by giving everyone guns."

How does Ariana know this? These details were left out of the story I've been told at home. Yet she speaks so confidently, as if she is explaining something even small children know.

Ariana, Rebecca and Josh speak in outraged whispers to

one another as my cheeks burn in embarrassment and anger. How could she call me a Nazi? Weren't all the Nazis dead?

I search the classroom for anyone who might have something to say, but everyone turns their eyes. My best friend Gabi looks thoughtful. Everyone else looks down at their desks. Did they all know this before—that the Autobahn was a means of killing more people, that he had put people to work by ensuring they eliminated others?

Even Mr. Schwertfeger looks flabbergasted. It seems like he is not prepared for this. He looks at his watch.

"Time is up," he says. "Please clean your desks."

Hot tears sting the backs of my eyes. I wish for someone to explain all this—to build the bridge between what Father has said and the new truth I am learning. But as I search the classroom for someone who will meet my gaze, I begin to doubt that this bridge can be built.

I don't dare turn around to look at Ariana, Rebecca or Josh. Relief tinged with despair floods me when the bell rings for recess.

For the next several days, I cannot meet Ariana's eyes in school. My gut twists whenever I see her. I have always liked Ariana. Her open face is kind, and although we are distant classmates, I've felt that we could be real friends. I've envied her too, for her friends and the close-knit community that hangs around her. Our school is known for having more Jewish kids than other schools in town; I watch how easy the Jewish students are with one another. They all know each other from temple and seem to have a group of built-in friends which I can only wish for. Now it appears that I will never have the chance to join Ariana's circle. To have offended her so disastrously tears me up; I am determined to do what I can to make things right.

One day Ariana comes to class in a dark blue velvet skirt and coat and a white blouse. She looks very nice; I decide this is my opportunity to undo my mistake from the other day.

I approach Ariana, who stands in the hall, talking to a classmate. "You look nice. I like your outfit."

"Thanks," Ariana says. She continues her conversation with the other girl.

"Sometimes I dress up too, for holidays. Is it a holiday?"

"Today is Rosh Hoshana. I'll leave school early today. Rebecca stayed home, but I wanted to come to school for a little while."

"Rosh Hosha . . . what's it called again?" I smile at Ariana.

"Rosh Hoshana," she repeats slowly. "Jewish New Year."

I make a mental note—I want to remember it. As I have learned since the Jewish Center visit, there are so many things I don't know. I want to understand more, the things Father will not share.

A man stands at the end of the hallway. He catches Ariana's eye and waves.

"That is my father," says Ariana. "I must go now."

I watch her go and hope that I have successfully broken the ice—that Ariana doesn't hate me forever.

As the day wears on, I feel I have crossed an invisible line. On the one side are the things Father has taught us. On the other are all the things I have learned since visiting the Jewish Center.

Father is right. Father is always right. He reads so many newspapers, is so esteemed in the community and among his friends—how could he be wrong? The Nazi regime had granted him a scholarship so that he might study in Erlangen to become a doctor. He had benefited from a government which chose to invest in its people. Perhaps that is why he chose to praise the Nazis when it seemed that the rest of the world despised them. Could I grant Father this understanding and stand with him on the ground that Hitler had done good things for Germany?

Until our visit to the Jewish Center, I hadn't fully believed that the prosecution of the Jews had taken place. Father said we shouldn't have watched the Holocaust miniseries. Over dinner after our visit, I was inclined to agree with him. A world in which he is wrong is a world where the sky isn't blue.

Yet the Jewish Center visit and documentary shook me to my core. It has only been a few days, but the pieces inside me rearrange themselves. Father's answers to my questions have not been satisfactory. He has tried to justify Hitler's killing of the Jews by saying that Stalin killed even more people, yet no one talks about that. Father has spoken of Mussolini and other authoritarian leaders of the twenties and thirties. Each time he changes the subject, I see more clearly what he is doing.

Recently, I read a book called *Friedrich*, about two boyhood friends who grew up in Germany between 1925 and 1942. Friedrich is Jewish; the narrator, who doesn't have a name, is Christian. The narrator tells of the horror Friedrich's family endured as the Third Reich came to power. In the last chapter, Friedrich dies in front of a bunker, killed by an air raid. Members of the neighborhood were safe inside the bunker and wanted to help him. Yet one neighborhood member—the block leader—was a Nazi. Everyone feared him; instead of helping Friedrich, the neighbors ducked and saved themselves.

I rewrite history in my mind. If the Jews had left after Kristallnacht, the Holocaust could have been avoided. If it had been me in that bunker and Ariana outside it, of course I would have helped her. I wouldn't have cowed to the Nazi; I would have rallied the neighborhood to save Ariana, and we would have overpowered the block leader. If I had been alive thirty years ago, I would have done what was right.

If, if, if, if.

18 GANGING UP

My worries at school are soon joined by worries at home. When I came home from school several weeks ago, Mother opened the door dressed in black, her face streaked with tears. Aunt Siegrid had died of Leukemia. She was only forty-four years old.

My thoughts drift to my first memories of Aunt Siegrid; I was three or four years old, and her husband had driven a horse-drawn carriage through our cobblestone streets to pick up Gerda and Elsa for a ride. The horses' hooves made click-clocking sounds on the street: Aunt Siegrid's husband sat high and happy on the carriage while their children, Katha and Matze, waved to us from a distance. I wanted to go with them so badly, to pet the beautiful brown horse, but I was too young and had to stay at home.

On our last trip to Aunt Siegrid's cottage on Sylt in the North Sea during spring break this year, Mother had not been there. Father had bounded to Aunt Siegrid's cottage as seagulls flew over our heads making their "keow" call—I could barely keep up with him. Aunt Siegrid had greeted us at the door with her beautiful, tanned face and her long, shoulder-length auburn hair—her pretty hair that was gone when I visited her with Mother at the hospital a few weeks ago.

I was not allowed to enter the room, but from the hallway, I saw her bold head laying on the pillow. I couldn't believe how sick she was. Since her husband had died, years ago, Aunt Siegrid, my honorary aunt, was always at our house. If Father had no other guests, she would be there: sitting in the living room with Mother and Father, smoking and drinking wine. I appreciated Aunt Siegrid's softening effect on my parents; they didn't chastise us when she was near.

Without Aunt Siegrid, there is a giant, gaping hole at the center of our family. Each day she is not in our home, Mother and Father seem to drift farther apart. They enclose themselves in their own worlds. No one shares their grief, but I see Mother more often with a face streaked by tears. I never see Father cry. I tiptoe around him. All that unspoken pain must be released somehow, and I wonder when the blow will fall.

I do not have to wait long before his anger and grief transform into something more dangerous. It is Sunday after church. Aunt Siegrid's funeral has been weeks ago. My family is gathered around the dining table in the living room. Mom has prepared one of her customary Sunday feasts. I eat in silence. I hope to remain unbothered and let my mind wander. I haven't seen Aunt Siegrid's children, Katha and Matze, since the funeral. How miserable they must feel. I only know that they are living with Aunt Siegrid's sister right now.

"How are Matze and Katha doing?" I ask.

The question makes Father uncomfortable. He shakes his head out of frustration while Mother answers, "They are furious with us. They say that we have stolen time with their mother—time that would have belonged to Matze and Katha. I believe that they don't want to see us again."

She looks so sad and eats her meal in silence. It makes sense to me because I remember that Katha was jealous of the time I spent with her mother. When I visited their house, she made fun of me. Once she fed me butter and pretended it was ice cream. "Taste it. Don't you see this is ice dream, you stupid girl!" Katha had laughed as she'd forced the spoon full of butter into my mouth. In another one of Katha's tricks, she made me go out into the street dressed as an old woman. Sometimes I was afraid of her and didn't feel safe in our "play"—but mostly, I loved Aunt Siegrid so much that I put up with it. Besides, I had no choice; Mother and Father said I must spend time with Katha so they could socialize with Aunt Siegrid.

"These potatoes need more salt," I hear Father grumble. His voice sounds like a wild lion locked up in a small cage. "The meat is not tender enough."

Mother ducks her head. So, she is the one to be singled out by Father today. Maybe she irritated him by releasing too much information to me about Aunt Siegrid. The mood had changed immediately when she had answered my question. Selfishly, I wonder if I will avoid a history quiz, as Father so often likes to do at the table to fill the silence—Charlemagne, Barbarossa, and the battle of the Teutoburg Forest. I can never answer questions to Father's satisfaction, so I recall Jesus's words: "Let this cup pass from me."

"You are right, Dad." Elsa chomps on the meat as if she chews a rubber tire. "The meat is too hard."

"I like the food." I softly say it to my plate. I hope it will be enough to get Father on a new subject.

"Look at how hoity-toity Mom eats." Now Father leans back in his chair, wearing an amused smile. He raises his fork and sticks out his pinky finger in imitation of Mom—although I have never seen her eat this way. Father purses his lips together, extra prissy. Elsa and Gerda laugh.

"Anne, please go get me a cigarette."

I jump to my feet and retrieve one, hand it to Father. He puts it in his mouth and signals that he wants me to light it too.

When I do, Father takes a deep breath and exhales smoke over the kitchen table. He studies us all. The safest thing to do is avoid Father's gaze, so that is what Mom does. Her head is bent over her plate as she continues eating in silence.

At last, Father's gaze lands on Elsa and Gerda. "You have inherited my eyes." He smiles proudly; my sisters beam back at him.

I know it is safer not to engage him—but of course, I want his warm smile to land on me too. "What about my eyes?" I can't resist asking.

Father studies my eyes. "Yours are okay too. But they are a mix. And Christiane, yours don't really have any color."

Mom keeps her head down over her plate.

"It is always better to have a pure color." Father's voice grows louder as he lectures. "Pure green, brown, or blue. Mixtures are not ideal."

Elsa and Gerda immediately examine each other's eyes, admiring their pure blue color. How I wish I shared this trait with them, that my ugly mixed eyes shone like dark blue gemstones as my sisters' do.

"I like your eyes, Mom." My voice shakes as I say it. "They look brown to me, not colorless."

"No," Father says harshly. "They look dead."

Elsa and Gerda chuckle; Father smiles. This is his idea of a "joke." Mom attempts a smile too, so I do as well. Maybe if we humor Father and laugh, he will move on?

"Christiane, you inherited those eyes from your mom."

"Omi Dina?" asks Gerda.

"Yes, she has also this mixture." Father's stare bores into the top of Mom's head like he is willing her to respond.

"I don't like my eye color," Mom finally admits.

"See." Father nods and leans back in his chair. He gestures to my sisters and me. "Your mom came from East Prussia. She has the high cheek bones typical of that region. She is the

Slavic type; they are stocky. It is better to have an oval face and to be tall." He gazes at Elsa, Gerda, and me and shakes his head. "You three have inherited the Slavic genes."

He says this as if we'd all had something to do with the choosing of our genes and had each made a grave mistake.

"During the Third Reich, the Aryan race was viewed as the leading race. I never asked them for anything. But they always promoted me because of my leadership and knowledge."

Now he is discussing the Aryan race—how they were viewed as industrious and ambitious—as he has done before. "The physical characteristics of an Aryan are blond hair and blue eyes." He looks at Elsa and Gerda, nodding his approval at my sisters' Aryan looks. "They have a slender face, high forehead, and a perfectly pronounced bump at the back of the skull."

In Hitler's Germany, Aryans were perceived as chivalrous, diligent, and tenacious. All good things were ascribed to the Aryan, or Nordic, type: they were heroic, calm, and ruthless when the need arose. Aryans also had the ability to entertain people with their storytelling, and they leaned more toward the sciences than the humanities. Aryans were competitive visionaries designed to lead others.

This is what Father has always told me. Yet in my mind, his image of the Aryans has been replaced by another: the Nazi soldiers plucking corpses from the back of a truck and hurling them into a mass grave.

Father glances at me. He must read the troubled look on my face. As if answering an unspoken attack, he says, "I was never a party member, though."

Father received all the benefits of Hitler's Germany—was an officer in Hitler's army, even—but was never a member of the Nazi party and didn't know about the mass extermination of the Jews. How could this be true?

Mother and I enter the kitchen to get dessert. As we spoon

fruit sauce over the ice cream, I study the back of her head. She lacks an "occupit" or a bony protuberance at the back of her skull. It disturbs her greatly; sometimes she mentions it when she does her hair in the morning. When she was pregnant with me, Mom's greatest fear was that I would inherit her blemish. Mom has told me that she palpated the back of my head when I was born; when she found the occupit, she breathed a sigh of relief.

What does it matter if someone has a bump at the back of their skull or not? How could that indicate superiority? I've never had that thought until today.

I've never had the thought until today.

"Ahh, the dessert is coming!" exclaims Father as Mother and I reenter the living room and put it on the table. Mother gives Father his bowl; he clucks. "Why are you always so scarce with the dessert? Get them more dessert!"

"Yes, Mother, we want more dessert!" demands Elsa.

Something in Mom has broken; she doesn't meet Father or Elsa's eyes. But I can see her cheek reddening and water pooling in her eyes.

"Why are you crying, Christiane?" Father will not stop. "Did we do anything wrong?"

"Yes, Mother, you're saying I do *everything* wrong!" yells Elsa, and Gerda and Father smile; they are having fun. "Isn't that right, Mom?"

Mom has said no such thing. In fact, she's said nothing at all.

"I will go and get ice cream," I say, desperate for some way to help Mom. I head into the kitchen and bring the ice cream container back. "See, now we can serve ourselves," exclaims Father.

"Why didn't you bring this out to start with?" Elsa demands of Mom. She spoons more ice cream onto her plate. "It's because you don't want us to gain weight. We're *starving*."

At that, Mom stands and leaves the table, her face streaked with tears. I long to follow her, to help in any way I can—but I am torn. If I leave, will my sisters and Father immediately start saying mean things about me? I am certain they will.

I remain sitting. Yet after everyone has left the table, I gather the dishes and take them into the kitchen. Cleaning up is the little help I can offer. I wish I could do more—spare her Father's attacks, help her reclaim her dignity. Yet in Father's house, I am powerless to stop he and my sisters from ganging up on Mom. He is the one who decides on whom his pleasure or displeasure falls. Today, Mom received the brunt of Father's lashing out; tomorrow it may be me.

I was beginning to see that this is how Father expressed the unsaid things inside him: his grief over Aunt Siegrid, his guilt about his involvement in the war and having survived it, his sadness over the loss of his own father in the First World War.

It is me, my sisters, and Mom who are left behind to clean up the mess.

19 TOUCHING THE WORLD OUTSIDE

It is 1979, I am almost thirteen, and things grow more tense in our house by the day. Father and Mother retreat into their own private worlds even further; when they speak, it is through harsh words—Father—or tears —Mother. As the atmosphere grows more tumultuous at home, the world outside does too.

One night in my bedroom, I open my diary to a long prayer I wrote when I was ten. Each line in the prayer was a response to some haunting fear; I'd written the line to neutralize the fear, so the prayer read like this:

To avoid the Russians taking over West Berlin: "Dear God, please let there be no war anymore. Amen."

In response to recent robberies in our neighborhood: "Dear God, don't let any robber ambush us or break into our house."

Then there were the bodily worries: "Dear God, don't let us become disabled."

Because I had been diagnosed as deaf in one ear, most likely due to mumps, and had recently read about Helen Keller: "Dear God, don't let us become deaf or mute."

After I discovered a book about drugs that portrayed an

opium addict as an Asian little person, so weak from the drug that he needed a stick to lift his entire upper body—and after my sisters had told me that strangers could offer me drugged candy: Dear God, don't let us have eaten drugs.

And the worries at school:

"Dear God, please let us get better in school in those classes we are not really good at."

"Dear God, please don't let me become unpopular in class."

"Dear God, please let my sisters get the permission to go to secondary school and to do well in the second semester."

"Dear God, please don't let me be frightened anymore."

When I was ten, Jesus had helped me with these fears, which gnawed like rats on my soul. I imagined him walking to school with me, his long white robe swaying over his sandals, brown hair falling gently around his shoulders. Everyone would be jealous of me, I thought; they'd wish that *they* had such a wonderful friend. Jesus always knew the right thing to do. He knew the right answer to a math problem I couldn't solve; he stood by me if one of my school mates spat in my face or hit me on the way home from school; he could remove the pain caused by my parents' constant quarrels.

I look at my prayer again. The last prayer reads in response to the Baader-Meinhof group, who had put West Berlin and West Germany for more than a decade into chaos by killing politicians and robbing banks: "Dear God, don't let any murderer blackmail or kidnap us. Amen."

Since my ten-year old prayer, the Baader-Meinhof group still poses a constant threat; in my mind, they had taken over the spot of "Bad Guys," once held exclusively by the Russians. Three years ago, I didn't know exactly what they wanted, only that my parents disapproved of their radical, militant ways. The group is angry about the conservative government in West Germany and how many ex-Nazis still held positions of power.

Back then, I remember the afternoon, my sisters and I

had gathered in front of the advertising column at the corner of our street. We studied the "Wanted Terrorists;" the long list of black and white headshots of the Baader-Meinhof group—also known as the Red Army Fraction (R.A.F.)—stared back at us. Ulrike Meinhof, the head of the group, had been crossed out. She had been captured a few years ago.

That was one point for the good guys.

What struck me back then while staring at the poster were the faces of the women. These were *educated* women, from conservative families like mine—now wanted for murder, bank robbery, and blackmail. My sisters and I stood at the edge of the street, discussing the missing fugitives' whereabouts with our friends, repeating what we'd heard from our parents and the media.

My ten-year old's fragile sense of security was rocked by the death of Ulrike Meinhof.

One day I came home from school and found Mom glued to the TV. My parents speak of TV as if it is a plague. But more and more, I found Mom gathered here, watching the unfolding political events. A reporter on the screen announced that Ulrike Meinhof had been found dead in her cell. I read shock on Mom's face.

"When she was still working as a journalist, Ulrike Meinhof lived and studied for a while in the Miquelstraße, not far away from our house. You know, around the corner where Aunt Siegrid lived." Mom kept her gaze on the TV. "Her father was a pastor. She was around my age."

I was surprised to hear Mom speak of a terrorist this way, as if she sympathized with her. Was there some part of Mom that saw herself in Ulrike Meinhof? Would they have become friends, before Ulrike became an outcast? Did Ulrike attend the same press ball that my parents attended every year?

On the other hand, Father viewed Ulrike's death as long overdue. At dinner, he pronounced: "This Ulrike Meinhof was a crazy woman. They took a X-ray of her skull after she had died and had found a tumor in her head. This might have contributed to her radicalism." Father pointed his index finger to his forehead and spins it in circles. "A woman who acts like her—so aggressive—must be a little cuckoo."

Even then as a ten years old, I wondered why they had examined her brain, it was like they wanted to solve the riddle how a woman could become such a threat, as if they wanted to proof that she was mentally ill. I just felt alienated about that procedure. Even though she took her own life, they still treated her like a monster.

I could see that Mom was not the only one who sympathized with the R.A.F. I heard from the news—and from my classmates—how Ulrike had spent her last two years in complete solitary confinement in a psychiatric ward, with no access to the outer world. She and other leaders of the group, like Thomas Baader and Gudrun Ensslin, had been on a hunger strike to improve their detention conditions. Sometimes their captors had forced food down their throats. Holger Meins had died during one of these feedings. Thomas Baader and Gudrun Ensslin, eventually committed suicide in the fall of 1977.

I couldn't help but consider the arguments of my classmates, whose parents ran homes less conservative than mine. Their parents were disturbed by the way the government handled the R.A.F members' trials. It was authoritarian, they said—like the former times. We have a democracy now; people are allowed to express their true thoughts. Yet most of the politicians who ran the trails had a Nazi past; to some, they stood like an impenetrable, unforgiving wall and punished anyone been born after the Second World War who questioned their past.

Now at age 13, three years later after my prayer, the old guard even now does not approve. It is like the Third Reich's cruel mindset still lingers among us. At least women are now allowed to work without their husbands' permission. But the young generation fights for world peace in view of the never ending arms race between the Americans and the Russians.

With their long hair, drug use, and free love lifestyle, the hippies are everything Father despises. At his evening dinner parties, Father rails against the youth movements and praises the conservative media.

I know what "hippies" look like. I was fascinated when we came across some of them standing on a street corner. One Sunday afternoon, we recently had visited the Luisenstädter cemetery in Kreuzberg on the other side of West Berlin, where Grandma Marie is buried, Father's mother, the one who I assume had died of sadness due to Grandpa's death in WWI.

Kreuzberg is a West-Berlin district, overcrowded it seems and like pressed against the wall. Here I can feel the Russians closeness. They are just behind the wall which at times appears on my right hand side while crossing some intersections and let me feel insecure. Kreuzberg is cheaper than our neighborhood, which is why so many workers, craftsmen, students, and young people who want to escape military service live there. As we drove through this district on our visit to Grandma Marie's grave, we passed shabby looking apartment buildings with banners hanging out of the windows that read NO WAR, or showed painted peace signs, the walls graffitied with words like SHIT, and other curse words. Cigarette stubs, old newspapers, and empty bottles lined the sidewalks in contrast to our neighborhood that is always cleaned up. I looked out the window of Father's Mercedes at the young hippies smoking and laughing with each other, strumming guitars or reading books as if they had no place else to be.

I couldn't square their poor living conditions with the expressions on their faces. The hippies looked happy.

"These young people are crazy and wild," Father grumbled. "They should go to East Germany and stay there if they don't like it here."

Another fascination was all the cultures that found a home in Kreuzberg. There were laborers from Turkey, Italy, and Greece who had come when the government offered low-paying jobs in the fifties. Driving through decades later, it was like Kreuzberg was its own little country; in fact, Kreuzberg had the nickname "Little Ankara." I couldn't take my eyes off the veiled Turkish women running errands and pushing strollers, surrounded by groups of students. Dark-skinned men sat at cafes smoking or eating Doener Kebab. When we drove by the Kreuzberg Park on Bergmann street, it looked like a lively party; children, young adults, and old people were surrounded by heavy smoke coming from their barbecues. I inhaled the delicious scent of grilled lamb.

Father never stopped at one of these places to try a Doener Kebab, and we didn't ask him to. But he encouraged me to look outside and to observe what was happening. I realized that he knew West Berlin like the back of his hand.

Looking back, I wondered—if Aryans were known for being heroic, what were other cultures known for?

I looked at the happiness of the Turks grilling in the park, the hippies existing joyfully and carefree on the street corners, and I wondered what did these people leave behind in order to start a life here in this town facing the wall every day and still being content?

This memory stays with me. Berlin has changed, and it will continue to change. *I* am changing. Each day I understand more; I see there is so much knowledge that has been kept from me in the closely guarded world that Father and Mom have built. I don't know whether to fear the change or leap into it. I wish my ten-year-old's prayer could protect me, but I've begun to doubt if Jesus works that way. I still love Jesus as much as ever, but he cannot save me from the creeping darkness in our home, how Mother and Father retreat into stony silences interrupted by bouts of Father's criticism and rage.

I feel trapped in our home, and another childhood story returns: Rapunzel. There must be a way for Rapunzel to climb out of the tower and be free. Her rescue comes through a prince—how might mine come?

I can only wait and see.

20 YPRES

Perhaps it is because things are changing so quickly that Father longs for the past. One day during spring break, Father announces that we will go to Ypres. "I am confident that we will find at least a trace of my father in that town," he announces.

I am not so sure. Father has made this trip to Ypres before, searching for his father, who died in the First World War. My grandfather's final resting place is a mystery. Each time Father takes this voyage and discovers nothing, his mood becomes even fouler than usual. My mother, sisters, and I pay the price.

Soon, we are driving through a rainstorm in West Flandern, Belgium. I sit in the middle of the back seat between Elsa and Gerda, once again relegated to the least comfortable seat in the car. Mom holds the map on her lap and strains to see the road through the downpour and swishing windshield wipers.

Engrossed in a book, *When Hitler Stole Pink Rabbit,* I don't mind the drive. It is about a young girl, Anna, who is forced to leave Berlin when Hitler comes to power. Anna chooses to take her stuffed dog on her voyage, rather than her beloved pink rabbit. When she learns that Hitler will stay in power and she cannot go back to her home, Anna claims that Hitler stole pink rabbit. Father's blue cigar smoke fills the car and burns my eyes.

Father does not know I have the book; I know he would be angry if he saw me, but I cannot put it down. When the car slows and we arrive in Ypres, I snap the book shut and put it in my backpack before Father can see.

I gaze out the windows. A heavy fog has settled over the town and sits between magnificent buildings. The fog makes it seems as if the town mourns the loss of something—though maybe I have simply attributed Father's feelings to Ypres itself.

"Let's get dinner," Father pronounces.

He chooses a restaurant across from the Gothic Cloth Hall, the famous center of town in Ypres. As we walk there, Father tells us how the Cloth Hall was one of the largest commercial buildings of the Middle Ages. I crane my neck to see its pointed turrets and spires.

Inside the restaurant, the smells of roast venison and red wine make me dizzy. A waitress seats my family; all around us are happy travelers, speaking in French and English. I recognize their calls of "Garcon, s'il vou plait!" or "Steward, another glass of wine, please." From what I can tell, we are the only Germans here. Father looks me in the eyes, then searches out my sisters. He says in a low voice,

"We have lost the war here twice."

I know something of this because Father has told us before. Here in Ypres were three major battles in the First World War, as well as a battle in the Second World War which gave an advantage to the Allied forces.

Father has said the words with bitterness, though he keeps his voice low:

"We have to be humble so as not to attract attention here," for fear that a waiter or restaurant patron will hear and judge our family. I would not blame them. Since my eyes have been opened, I want no part of Father's "we."

I gaze at the happy English and French families and envy them. They are boisterous, carefree: though this place has seen so much death and pain, they are the victors. Here they have nothing to fear.

Meanwhile, I grow more self-conscious about being German by the day. Father's "we"—the Germans—have been responsible for most of the catastrophic messes of the twentieth century. Did I see or imagine how the waitress's eyes darkened when she heard Father's German accent? I constantly fear that others will see or hear me and think only of Hitler.

Still, I'm aware of a deep unfairness. The French and English families may mourn their dead properly—that is the right of victors. The perpetrators in history are not allowed to grieve in the same way, and we were the instigators and losers. Yet Father's entire life has been shaped by the loss of *his* father, who fell in April of 1918, when Father was only three years old. My grandfather's death is what caused the permanent sorrow to set in Grandma Marie's bones; I remember the time we visited her at Christmas when I was a young child not long before she died and was buried on the Luisenstädter cemetery in Kreuzberg. I shook her cold, bony hand and her sadness crawled inside me, as if it were contagious. It is responsible for Father's lonely childhood. No one was ever able to heal the wound caused by the loss. Father's uncle had tried. His approach had been to feed Father's mind with knowledge—history, science, geography, and chess. In some respects, he had succeeded. But the wound to Father's soul stayed; over time, it had turned a part of him bitter and cold.

I recognize Father's behavior; it is how he acts when in the presence of a superior. He, who is usually so commanding at home—the head of a hospital—is now jumpy and awkward.

After the waitress takes our order, I try to think of something intelligent to say.

"I read that 3,000 young Germans died here in the First World War."

"Yes." Father nods, slow and grave. "Full lecture halls emptied. The young men ran to the battlefield, hungry for war. They thought it was an honor to die for their country. They believed the war would be over soon, and they would achieve a quick victory." He takes a swig of beer. "War is never that simple."

He looks over his shoulder to ensure no one has heard his speech. The mannerism reminds me of someone in battle, checking for the enemy behind his back. Father's instincts were forged in war.

We leave the restaurant and enter the foggy night. The air's wetness creeps into my clothes and let me shiver. When we pass the sombre Cloth House it seems to drown in a sea of yellow spotlights. Father guides us to an enormous gate. Made of bright marble, it illuminates its surroundings by itself. Once on the other side of this gate, the enemy—Germans—stood in wait. I think of the English soldiers who marched through, transporting canons on their way out onto the field and coffins on their way back.

The gate is called the Menin Gate. It is a memorial to the thousands of British soldiers who died here and were never found. I crane my neck to see the proud lion, which sits atop a marble sarcophagus rising from the arch's highest point.

Light from the street illuminates us and reflects from the walls of the nearby buildings. In the polished marble, I can see my long shadow.

Suddenly, Gerda pinches my arm. When I turn to her, she nods her head toward a sea of names engraved in the gate's walls: the missing. Inside the gate's huge arch, there are more than 50,000 names.

All that misery and loss weights me down like chain armor around my shoulders. My family is silent. Is it because each of us is taking in the enormity of such a loss? Or because we don't want to be overheard by the English and French tourists who surround us?

We don't share our thoughts, so there's no way to know.

The next day, the fog lifts and so do my spirits as my family heads to the German cemetery in Langemark, a few miles north of Ypres. Here, we'll be able to talk more freely, without fear of being overheard by the British and English tourists.

A heavy red sandstone building stands at the entrance of the cemetery. The oak trees have yet to bud, in these last days of Belgian winter. Shiny blue-black ravens rest on their massive, naked branches and welcome us with a *kraa, kraa.*

Father hurries eagerly through the gate. "It must be right here, behind the entrance."

He is so sure of success this time—of finding his father—despite his previous failings. I trail behind, distracted by the brown and withered leaves which cling to a giant oak tree and have survived the winter. The wind off the Atlantic picks up and tugs at the leaves. They resist separation, flapping like flags on a sailboat—all but one, which gives into the wind's power and floats away, lighter than air. I watch the leaf's swirling, gracious fall to the wet ground, where it is promptly soaked. Someone crushes the leaf underfoot.

Someone crushes the leaf underfoot.

Mother's voice comes from farther down the path. "Come here, quickly! I found him!"

I rush to Mom, who bends over a register that contains the names of soldiers buried here. Father and Elsa flank her; I peek between them. Father lets out a sigh.

"Your uncle," he grumbles.

"Yes," Mom says. I can hear the excitement in her voice, but also the caution. She musn't be *too* excited. After all, we have come here on Father's mission. Mother speaks to Elsa, Gerda, and me.

"Uncle Heinrich. He was my father's older brother who died in 1915."

Omi Dina had told me the story; Heinrich had been my Opi's older brother, the golden boy and successor to the publishing house run by Opi Helmuth's parents. Heinrich had died on my grandfather's birthday. From then on, the day was one of mourning.

"Let me have a look." Father pushes to the front of the small desk, his eager eyes scanning the register. Elsa stays close to him.

Mom purses her lips, irritated. She soon leaves the building. I follow her onto a wide lawn with no flowers. Gerda walks alone, wandering through the rows of headstones and gazing intently at each engraved name. It is a blessing, at least, that all these young men can now be gathered in this quiet place and rest in peace forever. That is the comforting story I tell myself.

Mom stops right behind the "Kameradengrab," of the graves of the missing. The grave is decorated with a wreath of oak leaves surrounded by eight escutchons; each represents the Belgian regions where Germans had fought.

"Maybe they buried him in here," she muses.

Father strides toward us, then comes to an abrupt stop.

"I think that we have seen enough here."

Our search here is over, almost as soon as it has begun. This is how Father is; once he loses his patience with an endeavor, it ends. The irritation in his voice masks the disappointment I see in his eyes.

"Let's at least look at two more sides. Perhaps my search will pay off at one of them."

Mother joins Father, and they link arms and walk to the car.

It is the most affection I have seen them show one another in months—years? Perhaps there is something about this place, which holds the memories of people they have both lost, which draws them together. Perhaps they will remain close, even back in Berlin.

    I linger behind my parents and sisters and look at the oak tree to count the remaining brown leaves—but there are none. The wind has swept them all away as we've searched.

21 SHE IS GONE

When we return to Berlin, my hopes for a reconciliation between Mother and Father are dashed.

One day I come home from school and am greeted by Rahni, our housekeeper. This is strange; usually Rahni stays busy dusting, arranging flowers, or cleaning silverware. Rahni takes my backpack and anorak, then bends to whisper in my ear:

"Your mother has gone away." Her eyes crinkle in sympathy for me.

Though Rahni's expression is strange, I don't think much about what she has said. Mother has gone away—she will return. When? Perhaps by dinnertime, maybe tomorrow morning.

What I don't admit to Rahni is that it's a relief to have Mother gone, however briefly. It seems that lately I can do nothing right in her eyes. Mother's criticism has been constant: about my figure, how long it takes me to reply when she asks me a question, what I eat. If Mom has gone, at least she has taken her disapproval with her.

My ears prick at the sound of Father's whistling. He has come home early from work.

"Anne!" Father calls me from his study. "Come here."

I go to Father's study and enter, cautious, ever the mouse in the presence of the big cat. Elsa is there too, lolling on the gray sofa. Immediately, I am struck by a sense of wrongness. I crawl under Father's oak desk and find Gerda there. It seems that we've both chosen to hide from the truth, whatever that might be.

I hear the click of Father's cigarette lighter above me. "Your mother is gone."

Those strange words from Rahni, repeated again. What can they mean? I crawl out from under the desk and study Father's face, remind myself to keep breathing.

"What does it mean?" Elsa, all business, asks what I am thinking.

"I don't know. I assume that she went to Wilhelmshaven and is staying with your Aunt Bettina."

Wilhelmshaven is more than five hours away. All right, I think. She will be gone for a few weeks. Immediately, my mind rationalizes Mother's departure and plan for her return.

Father interrupts my thoughts. "I don't think she is coming back soon."

So, more than a few weeks? A month or two?

"I want you to call her right now and ask her to come home." Father puffs on his cigarette. "She has three daughters who need her."

I cannot tell who the "you" is. Elsa, Gerda, or I? Father addresses the room at large as if he speaks to an adult who is not present. Shouldn't calling Mom be *his* job?

I recall Father and Mom's arms threaded together at the German cemetery north of Ypres. I had thought it meant something; perhaps that they were both willing to love each other, to try harder in their marriage.

I cannot believe how wrong I was.

The grains of the oak run in long lines down Father's desk, like trenches. The lines remind me of the crinkles in Gerda's blankets. Last week, Elsa, Gerda, and I had sat on her bed, and...

The memory makes my breath catch in my throat. I relive each painful detail.

Elsa had been complaining: "Mom is so mean. She always criticizes how I eat and my table manners. Besides, she's dumb. I've had it with her stupid diet plan."

Mom had put Elsa and Gerda on a strict diet of eight hundred calories a day. This was, supposedly, meant to heal my sisters' congenital dermatitis. Yet the plan had created a kind of neurosis in my sisters—especially Elsa, who now weighed each salad leaf before eating it. She becomes smaller and smaller before our eyes.

Elsa sat straight up on the bed; a wicked look came over her. "Eat this butter or starve!" Elsa said in a shrill voice, in imitation of Mom.

Gerda and I fell back laughing, to Elsa's delight.

"Put your spoon down! Sit up straight!"

I chimed in. "Answer quickly when I ask you a question—your answer must come as quickly as an arrow from a bow!"

We laughed so hard, we did not notice the door had opened. Yet something drew our attention to the doorway, and there stood Mom. Hurt and jealousy mingled in her face. I thought of all the times I had been jealous of the intimacy between Elsa and Gerda and knew in a second how she felt.

My stomach dropped.

She stared at us for several agonizing moments. "I thought you were doing your homework."

Elsa grinned mockingly. "We're almost done. Besides, we wanted to talk."

"I want you to finish right now," Mom said, her voice quiet.

"Stop criticizing," Elsa spat. She pursed her lips into a thin line as her eyes grew frantic—a sign that trouble was on the way.

"Start right now. It is almost time for dinner." Mother's lips were a thin line too.

"No." Elsa sneered. "We won't do it. And besides,"—Elsa's voice raised to a high pitch—"we don't love you. Never did."

Her words were like a rifle blast ringing through the room. Mom staggered. When she regained herself, she looked to Gerda, then me.

I wished I could distance myself from that "we." The same way I wished I could distance myself from Father's statement in the Ypres restaurant: "*We* lost the war here twice."

But I nodded my consensus with Gerda. Elsa was too powerful to be denied.

Mother turned without a word, then headed out of the door frame and down the hallway. Silence hung in the air. Elsa finally broke it.

"Well, it's true." She shrugged. "We don't love her."

With the memory tugging at my heart, I return to the present: in Father's study, his smoke hanging over everything. "You are going to call her," Father continues. "But don't tell her I asked you to call."

With a sigh, Elsa heads out of the room. Though Father has not identified who should call, Elsa has taken the job upon herself. Gerda and I follow her to Father's bedroom, where Elsa picks up the phone on Father's nightstand. She dials the number for Aunt Bettina and Stefan's house.

Gerda and I lean our heads together and try to hear. The phone rings; my heart beats faster. Then, Mom's voice comes on the line.

"Hello." She sounds unsurprised, as if she's expected us.

"It's us," Elsa says. "When are you coming back?"

"I don't come back."

Mom has walked out of our home as if it is the grocery store. It can't be true—a mother can't just *leave* her daughters.

Feelings ram together in my chest and fight for prime position. There's anger, at Mother and at Father—why couldn't he call himself and find some way to tell us the terrible news? There's sadness, the suddenness of loss. I am furious with myself for thinking that Mom and Father's closeness in Belgium signified a change in our house. I am mad at Elsa. Can't she make her voice more kind? Is there something she could say to bring Mom back?

And there is fear. Now we are stuck. Elsa, Gerda and I have no buffer to protect us from Father. When he is angry, we will be the only ones on whom he can release his rage.

What are we to do?

My confusion only grows when, a few days later, Gerda and I sit on the white wool carpet in her room. A magazine clipping of ABBA—whom Gerda loves as much as I love Jesus—smiles down at us. Gerda and I eat chocolate bars from the new Aldi grocery store when Gerda leans close to me and says:

"By the way, I knew Mom was leaving."

I swallow my bite of chocolate. "What do you mean?"

"She told me about it and wanted my opinion. She wanted to take me with her, but we decided it would be too complicated to change schools." Gerda wipes her mouth. "Maybe I'll join her later."

I try to make sense of my sister's words. "Do you want to live with Mom?"

Gerda only shrugs.

My stomach drops. I have done something wrong—I *must* have. All those times I had wanted to support Mom but hadn't because of my fear. How had Gerda been there for her when I was not? If I had acted differently, would Mom have chosen me?

It is not that I *want* to live with Mom. It is that I long to be chosen, as Father has chosen Elsa and Mom has chosen Gerda. The old story of Rapunzel in her tower returns to me. Rapunzel waited trapped in the tower, year after year, until at last the prince chose her; together, they found their way to freedom.

Who will be the one to choose me?

PART 3

22 MOM LEFT LONG AGO

Father cannot do without a woman to take care of the details of his life. Before long, one enters the picture.

The weekend after Mom's departure, I leave the house to drive my bike to the tennis club and nearly step on a tray placed in front of our doorstep. The tray contains a delicious-looking breakfast, with a vase of orange forget-me-nots in the middle. I later learn that Sister Lisa placed the tray there.

Sister Lisa's is Father's number one nurse—Father's number one sycophant—at the hospital. Her fiancé died in the Second World War; she has remained single ever since. Over the years, she has drawn closer and closer to Father. Though Lisa is kind to me, I can't help but dislike her.

Lisa is submissive and anxious. She clenches her teeth and makes a hissing sound when she laughs, as if she is scared to release more air, make more noise. What makes this worse is that she laughs often, for no apparent reason. It is a nervous habit that tries my patience.

The breakfast services soon become a regular weekend feature. Lisa, in her late forties, is diligent and demure and seems to have only one aim: to serve Father. She embodies the spirit of the BDM, or Bund Deutscher Mädchen—League of German Girls—though she is a woman and not a girl. The BDM was the female wing of the Hitler Youth—although they have long since disbanded, many view their ideals as the proper ones for German women. Father holds this view.

I detest all that they stand for, perhaps because I cannot think of the BDM without thinking of Lisa.

With Mom gone and Lisa filling in the gaps, a memory has come back to me—one I didn't even know I had.

Mom had left once before, when I was three years old. A woman named Sister Brigitte had looked after us then. I woke up in the morning and found her there one day, inexplicably.

"Where is Mom?"

"She comes back soon," Sister Brigitte had answered. "She needs a rest from all of you."

Sister Brigitte had fed my sisters and me and put us to bed, exactly as Mom would have. Several days later, Father drove us to a small lake where we visited a woman who lived in an apartment with wooden floors. The smell of violins greeted us, rich and woody. I gazed at the lake through the large front window while Father talked to the woman who took care of his violin.

Later, Father walked us to the lake. The air was cold enough for me to see my breath. I gazed at the ducks and swans when Father pointed at a hotel on the other side of the water.

"Look up!" Father said. "There's Mom on the balcony. Can you see her? Let's wave."

I looked in the direction which Father pointed. Was that really her? There she was, a distant figure waving silently. I waved like Father had told me, but I was confused. Why didn't she come down to see us?

"Mom called earlier today," Father said. "She misses you. She is coming back next week." But even at that age, I was not really sad that Mother stayed away from us, she always seemed distant, occupied with other things,

The memory strikes with the suddenness of a lightning bolt. If I could not stop Mom's leaving when I was three, perhaps it is wrong to believe that I could stop her now. What I envy is her choice: the choice to simply walk away from our house—Father's house—and the deep well of sadness within it. Is she happy now?

I doubt that happiness could be so simple. Still, I'd like the chance to see for myself.

As it turns out, I am the first person who will see Mom again. In May of 1980, I am invited to the confirmation of my favorite cousin, Caroline, in Goettingen. I need a new dress for the occasion. Rose Drache, our glamorous neighbor, has offered to take me shopping.

I cannot help but feel self-conscious as I sit next to Mrs. Drache in her white VW convertible. Her hair and makeup are always arranged perfectly. Since I have known Mrs. Drache, she hasn't changed a bit—she is always beautiful and perfectly self-possessed. Next to her, I feel ungainly and awkward.

My body has begun to morph in ways I can't account for. I feel myself rise like a yeast cake—all those chocolate bars Gerda and I sneak in her bedroom are finally showing. When I stand in front of the mirror, I don't know what to think of my changing body. Next to Mrs. Drache, I feel like I'm the ugly duckling, and she's the swan.

Mrs. Drache takes me to a fancy boutique near the Kurfürstendamm. She plucks a red dress from the rack with small flowers and frills on the sleeves.

"Look at you!" Mrs. Drache exclaims. "Your mom will be so happy to see you in this dress."

A boutique assistant is drawn by Mrs. Drache's praise. "Yes," the young girl nods. "It is beautiful."

I cannot tell if Mrs. Drache and the assistant are telling the truth. *Beautiful*—do they mean it? Lately, I've drawn more into myself. I study others. My goal is to determine their true feelings about me. Am I ugly or beautiful? Smart or stupid? Clever or dull?

I live in fear that people will think badly of me. If I disagree—say the dress is *not* beautiful, that I look strange—will Mrs. Drache not like me anymore?

"Yes," I agree. "The dress is beautiful!"

After I change into my normal clothes, Mrs. Drache happily pays for the dress. If I had gone shopping with Sister Lisa, I would have ended up with a smock in a dull color, like gray or navy blue. At least this one is better.

On the Sunday morning of Pentecost—Caroline's confirmation day—the trees in my grandparents' garden bloom pink, white, and purple. A breeze wafts their scent to everyone gathered there. Even though it is Caroline's day, I feel as if all eyes are on me. The scandal of Mom's leaving hangs on me like a rotten scent. Surely, all my family members know what has happened—though no one speaks of it. Do I imagine that people turn quickly from me when they see me approach?

When I finally speak to Caroline, who is busy greeting all her guests and being the center of attention, she whispers in my ear, "Don't you want to talk to your mom?"

"Yes," I answer. Though the truth is, I don't know.

I'd written Caroline to tell her about Mom's leaving; she hadn't responded. I'd wondered about her silence and craved my cousin's support. Perhaps her parents, Mom's brother, and his wife, had told her not to get involved.

Caroline and I sit on a bench and smile while Aunt Bettina takes our picture. "You both look so nice."

I hope she means it. But as always, I doubt the sincerity of the compliment. I cannot simply accept someone's kindness as truth.

"Christiane," Aunt Bettina calls to Mom. "Look at Caroline

and Anne. Would you like to sit next to Anne? I will take a picture of you two."

As Mom walks toward the bench, I sense all eyes on me and wish the ground would open and swallow me. My red dress feels too tight. I feel itchy and stupid.

Mom settles herself on the bench. "Who bought you that dress?"

"Rose Drache." Aunt Bettina's camera goes *click, click, click*. I am an actor in the world's most awkward play.

"Do you know that I have found an apartment in Wilhelmshaven?"

Does she want congratulations? "Yes, Dad told me."

Mom takes my arm. *Click, click, click.*

"I am working as a stand-in doctor in Braunlage for a couple of weeks."

This surprises me. It has been so long since Mom has used her medical degree, I wonder if she is even allowed. Does she command the clinic in Braunlage the way Father commands his hospital and home?

But I will not give her the satisfaction of asking questions. "Mmh."

Aunt Bettina smiles and nods, as if willing us to keep the conversation going. I look down at my feet. My white socks are dirty; I ran with my cousin Wilhelm through the bushes before the confirmation ceremony began. We ran in this way when we were children. I feel an ache, a longing to return to that time.

"It is good to see you." Mom slips her arm through mine and smiles.

Why did you leave? What happens next? I want to scream.

Deep inside, I know that Mom left long ago—long before her escape to Wilhelmshaven. There is no real bond between us. Bitterness seizes me. On the ride back to Berlin, I think of what I would like to say to her:

Your absence doesn't hurt because you were never a real mother.

You were too busy coping with your own deficiencies to protect us from Father.

Father is cruel, but at least he doesn't leave. He makes sure we will survive.

You enjoyed being the grand dame, the mistress of our house, the esteem that comes with being Father's wife. You cared more about that than you did about us.

You beat us, and you agreed to let Father do it, and that is just as bad.

I think of my constant nightmares—of the men in my room and other terrors—from my early childhood. Those nightmares form my earliest memories. Mom had offered protection then; she'd said I could sleep in her bed. I had denied her even as a young child.

I congratulate myself for my four-year old wisdom. Even then, I could see who Mom really was.

23 HOW TO FREE RAPUNZEL

Yet even with my bitter thoughts toward Mom, I miss her presence. Sister Lisa has swiftly taken Mom's place, with no discussion or input from my sisters and me. We drive in the family Mercedes to Sattelpeinstein, I in the middle of the back row like always. This time, Sister Lisa has packed our car picnic, exactly as Mom used to: cheese sandwiches and apples. Did Father give her this instruction? The blatant imitation disgusts me. Sister Lisa could have at least used a little imagination and packed different food.

Throughout the car ride, I stare at the back of Sister Lisa's head—her tight bun—as we drive down the freeway. Last time we'd made this drive, it had been only Mom and my sisters: no father. Mom was never one to follow speed limits. She sped down the highway, heading to Omi and Opa's, and was promptly pulled over by a policeman. The policeman lectured Mom in his thick GDR dialect about her wrongdoing while the typical GDR smell, evolving from his uniform, penetrated our car. Mom pulled off a masterful performance; she turned wistful and flirtatious, telling the policeman that she was headed to a funeral and was late. My sisters and I exchanged looks in the back seat; we were impressed with Mom's acting.

The policeman wasn't. He made Mom pay the one hundred Deutsche Marks fine, right then and there. Mom muttered about the policeman the rest of the drive, the greedy GDR officers who had nothing better to do than pop out unsuspecting and spring fines on innocent travelers. She later repeated the story to Opi and Omi, and we all commiserated about the wrongness of the socialist system, how corrupt the GDR officers were. Mom had left my sisters and me with one final admonition: Don't tell Father. We hadn't; I'd delighted in the secret.

I scowl at Sister Lisa and try to imagine her pulling off such a cunning trick. Sister Lisa would never—she is too demure, too nervous, and not nearly quick-witted enough.

"I always wanted to be either a nurse or a mother," Lisa says from the front seat. "I am so fortunate that I get to be both!"

Her nervous laughter is met with silence from the car.

Sister Lisa claiming a place as my mother—the thought sickens me. What would that life be like?

Images fill my head: Sister Lisa would ensure my sisters and I have a proper BDM education, that we are the perfect German girls trained to serve the men in our lives. We would clean the house spick and span while singing German hiking songs. Then we would sew, darn socks, cook hearty meals, and wait patiently for Father to come home to a well-ordered household.

I do not yet know what I want for my life; yet when I think of such a future, a pit forms in my stomach. *Not that,* my mind pleads.

When we arrive in Sattelpeinstein, Father and Sister Lisa spend the night in separate rooms. A small mercy.

The thought of a future as a perfect League of German Girls woman is unbearable to me, so I'm left wondering—what kind of woman am I supposed to be?

The models I've had leave me wanting. There is Mom, who could never speak out against Father: her anger and criticism and cruelty trickled down to us kids, until she could not bear her own sadness anymore and left. There is Sister Lisa, who acts like a nervous young child even though she is in her forties. Aunt Siegrid was graceful, beautiful, and seemed free—but she is dead. Is that the price women have to pay for independence?

When you get married, everything will be forgotten.

Aunt Anna's words from so long ago return to me now. She'd said them so simply, as if on my wedding day, a magic wand would wipe away the past. On that fateful day, I will automatically know how to behave: how to love and be loved by a husband, how to raise a perfect family. I want this for my future—yet it is not *all* I want. I've seen the bitter fruits of a life of servitude to husband and children: anger, depression, loneliness. There must be more for me.

I have almost no experience with boys. At Christian Achter's birthday party, someone had turned out the lights. Christian grabbed me and pulled me against his chubby body; I'd screamed when he'd forced his tongue into my mouth and moved it around like a slimy slug.

Elsa has roped me into "practicing kissing" in her bedroom, Hall and Oates playing from the American station on her radio. Elsa has told me to "think about something romantic" during these practice sessions. I don't have experience with romance, only with fantasy. So, my mind turns to fantasy.

Lately, I've begun to exchange my fantasies about Jesus for fantasies of Winnetou. Winnetou is the fictional leader of the Apaches; the author Karl May has written novels about him, and those books have been turned into movies. We watch them on the television with Father. I cannot turn from the TV on those movie nights—I am entranced by the actor Pierre Briece's sunburned skin and flowing black hair. A life-sized poster of Winnetou hangs above my bed and is the first thing I see every morning, as the film's searing music fills my ears and heart. Winnetou kneels in the dirt of the prairie and looks off into the distance, his silver rifle held upright.

In my fantasies, Winnetou's love interest is named Jane. Jane has morphed into a beautiful teenager with long blond hair—me, as I long to be. Jane and Winnetou sneak off to do secret, hot things. They've created a world of their own making and aren't concerned about what others think.

I'm not sure which part of the Winnetou fantasy captures me most—being passionately in love or being free. Winnetou and Jane roam the prairie and answer to no one. Is that a possibility for grown-up life? Not to serve a domineering man and wait on children, not to live in fear of a raging husband—does such freedom exist? The thought of being in control of my own life, joyfully sharing that life with a man who sees me as equal. It is intoxicating. But I am not sure if it is just another fantasy.

24 SEARCHING FOR OPTIONS

Maybe it is Winnetou, riding his horse through Western prairies, who fills me with dreams of America. Just like my dreams for my future married life offer visions of escape. The American fair happens every summer in the American sector of Berlin. Father takes my sisters and me there on a Wednesday evening, every year without fail. The American fair seems to offer an entire world of fun and fantasy. Ferris wheels, carousels, big dippers, ghost trains—so many rides, and Father lets us ride on any that we like.

American songs and excited laughter fill the air; the streets fill with families, young couples, and G.I.'s. I inhale the delicious scent of barbeque mingled with beer and popcorn and candy—for me, no trip to the American fair is complete without a ream of cotton candy melting on my tongue. Mickey Mouse, Goofy, and Donald Duck walk through the crowds and pose with happy locals and American soldiers, who must be homesick. Of course they miss America; why would anyone ever want to leave their country?

To me, America is a utopia. I notice how diverse the Americans are. It doesn't seem to matter what color their skin tone is, where they were born, whether they have the all-important occupit Father so prizes—every American seems to have equal opportunity. What's more, they can be proud of their country. They won the war and stopped Hitler; they don't carry around the shame of being German that never leaves me.

My school friend Gabi has an older sister who married an American G.I. and moved to San Diego. Gabi brought me a candle from California—the most beautiful candle I'd ever seen. It was made up of several beautiful colors and came in a glass holder. The candle was so beautiful I didn't light it for several weeks.

Still, I never showed the candle to Father. Despite his indulgence toward my sisters and me at the American fair, I sense his ambivalence toward America. American soldiers, along with French and British, live alongside us in West Berlin. They are there to support us in the event of a Russian invasion. Father is grateful to the Americans for liberating us from Russia in 1949. The Russians had sealed off access to West Berlin for 324 days; yet the Americans, led by General Clay, had airlifted food and supplies into West Berlin, keeping its citizens from starvation until the Russians finally gave in. Father speaks warmly of General Clay and the logistical feat of the airlift.

Yet Father is bitter about America too. "We would have won the war had it not been for the Americans." I have heard him say this on more than one occasion.

That *we*—I push back against it in my mind every time. Father speaks of how the Americans left no stone untouched in the Germany he loves and fought for—how they brought the land of poets and thinkers to its knees.

Father has taken us to every museum in West Berlin, but he never brings us to the Allies Museum on Clay Boulevard. I've heard that the museum talks about the Allied victory and how these victors have influenced German culture. There is a section on the Holocaust and the liberation of the concentration camps as well.

If we ventured to the Allies museum, would Father still be able to deny knowing about the six million murdered Jews? I sense his guilt, the knowledge that he was on the indefensible side of history, and his unwillingness to admit it and begin the process of redemption. And so Father's treatment of the Americans remains steeped in ambiguity, which I cannot help but pick up on. Although I dream of America, I don't imagine myself building a life there as Gabi's sister has. The American way of life seem to me too easy going and it is so far away.

Instead, I look for a means of escape that seems more reachable than either America or romance: religion.

"Don't you want to come with me to the meeting?" Gerda asks me one afternoon. "There's lots of nice people in the congregation. We'll have dinner together and talk. You'll see."

Gerda has recently joined the Free Christ congregation. The people there seem to fill her with something she can't get at home, something that is all her own. No longer are she and Elsa joined at the hip; they have each begun to spin in their own orbits. Elsa's orbit has her looking thinner by the day; she clearly has a problem with her eating, though no one talks about it. I worry about my sister. I'm glad Gerda has found something healthier to fill her time and thoughts, even if I resist going to the congregation myself.

It's not that I dislike Jesus; I still like him as much as ever. It's that I'm suspect of the Free Christ people. They meet in an apartment building in Charlottenburg and don't own a church building, which I find suspicious.

Nevertheless, I agree. Perhaps I'll find something to enjoy with Gerda and her new religious friends. Spending time with them should at least be more entertaining than staying at home.

"I'll go," I announce to Gerda, who beams from ear to ear.

I try to share in Gerda's enthusiasm, but the gloominess of the meeting hall dampens my spirits. The apartment building is sandwiched in between other high-rises; almost no light seeps in through the windows. This dreariness is matched by the people in attendance. They chat quietly and eat overcooked food. I scan the faces of the crowd and look for someone I could have a conversation with.

Who here likes Winnetou? I call out in my mind. *Is anyone obsessed with the Bay City Rollers, like me?*

But no one approaches me to start a conversation, and I feel too shy to start one myself. The congregants sit around the dinner table and make small talk, which is unbearable to me. I sit quietly and eat my dinner until a woman on my left with gray hair interrupts my solitude.

"Who do we have here?"

"This is my little sister Anne," Gerda says from across the table. "Anne, this is Gertrude."

I give Gertrude a close-lipped smile. I try my best to inject warmth into it, but I'm sure my face betrays my discomfort. I know how I appear to others. I've often been accused of being cold and difficult to approach; truthfully, I don't know how to insert myself naturally into situations where others have established a rhythm. Today is no different.

"Ah," says Gertrude with a warm smile. "Very nice to meet you."

I gaze longingly at Gerda, who is caught up in conversation with a young man whose beard almost covers his face. Wolf, I think. Gerda has mentioned him before. Wolf speaks with narrowed eyes, a focused intensity which Gerda seems to match. Occasionally, she interrupts his speech, and he nods.

Aha, I think. *This is why Gerda likes church.*

I hate Wolf right away, if only because he has Gerda's complete attention while I feel adrift in this sea of strangers.

I'm rescued at last from my awkwardness when someone says, "Let's pray."

Everyone stands and remains silent for a few minutes. If I can't talk to anyone here, at least I can talk to God.

Dear God, I pray. *Show me a sign that you exist. Please, may my parents get back together and be happy.*

"Amen," someone murmurs, and we all sit down again. Apparently, this is the end of the meeting, because soon everyone is talking. Gertrude has started a conversation with someone more interesting than I; they chat animatedly. My longing and awkwardness turn to frustration; I glance to my watch. How much longer must I be here?

What do you want to get home for?

My mind floats the question, and my heart sinks. I know there is nothing for me at home, just like there is nothing for me at the Free Christ congregation. At least I tried. I go find Gerda, tap her on the shoulder.

"I'm going home now."

"Already?"

"Dad is coming home soon," I stammer.

"*And?*"

"And he wants someone to be home when he gets there."

Gerda rolls her eyes. "I don't care."

It's a lame excuse, I know. Each step on my journey home I wonder if I've made the right decision. I will be alone at home, just as I was alone in the congregation. Is this how it will always be?

But it's clear to me; what Gerda has found in the Free Christ church—community and acceptance and love—I must search for somewhere else.

25 A HOUSE OF SECRETS

At home, I see less and less of my sisters. They will be in twelfth grade soon; I will be in tenth. My sisters will finish high school, and I will be left alone with Father.

Even now, I am home alone with Father most of the time. It is my duty to wait on and entertain Father, so I do. My fear of him is mixed with respect and an outsize desire to please. I prepare food for Father and sit with him at the dinner table, even though I long to escape into my own room. Father has said it is a woman's job to entertain men and ask them intelligent questions; I try my best to be interesting. Besides, if I do not, Father will lash out. He is sixty-four and works sixty hours a week at the hospital, as he tells us often. The least my sisters and I can do is offer him company.

I remain, glued to the house like a magnet to a metal plate. Except Gabi, I don't have other close friendships anyway. When classmates ask me to spend time with them, I decline. The duty I feel toward Father compels me to wait on him, and I can't bear the guilt trip he lays on me when he is not properly attended to.

In Mom's absence, life continues. Father doesn't ask me about the trip to Goettingen for Caroline's confirmation. As far as I know, he and Mom have not spoken at all. Sister Lisa spends the weekends at our house and sleeps in the guestroom. Father's music evenings continue; Frau Müller, our housekeeper, prepares the food for Father's guests. Elsa, Gerda, and I take turn serving snacks and waiting on the guests. Each Saturday, I make a cake, as Mom used to. Father discusses the merits and failings of each cake at length before taking his habitual Sunday afternoon nap. Father's world proceeds as normal with the women of the house waiting on his every need.

One late summer evening, I am home alone. I glance at the clock; Father will be home any minute. Working quickly, I slice meat and cheese and put bread on the table. At 7:30 p.m., Father's key turns in the lock. My stomach clenches; I hope Father will not see that I have just set out his dinner and lecture that I should have prepared it earlier.

Father glances to me as he walks through the door. "Good evening."

"Good evening."

"Thank you for preparing dinner."

I breathe a sigh of relief. No lecture tonight. Or at least if there is one, dinner will not be the subject.

Father heads straight to the refrigerator and pulls out a beer. We sit at the table in our usual chairs, I across from him. I watch him eat in silence; when he is finished, I fetch him a cigarette and light it. I long to escape to my room, where I can lose myself in the pages of a book.

"What are your plans for the future?" Father stares at me through squinted eyes.

I grimace. I *hate* it when he begins this line of questioning.

"I don't know," I stammer. "After high school, I want to go to university."

Father exhales sharply and shakes his head. He doesn't like this answer, as I knew he wouldn't. I don't know what my future holds; Father has it all planned out. I brace myself as he gears up for his monologue.

"Your grades are not even good enough for a high school degree."

He is right about that; since Mom has gone, they've dropped dramatically.

"You should finish high school after the tenth grade. Then you can become a secretary or something you don't need a high school degree for." He studies me, appraising. "You will find a husband soon, I guess. Of course, the moles on your right arm —they decrease your value. Yet I'm sure we can find someone to marry you despite them. And your snub nose." Father wrinkles his eyebrows. "It would be better if your nose were straight. Ah, well. Yet some man will not mind, probably." He smiles.

Until Father had pointed out my moles and snub nose, it had not occurred to me to be self-conscious about them. Now I desperately wish I could change them, even though Father's picture of my future fills me with a bleak dread.

I have never had a boyfriend, yet Father is planning my marriage. I long for romance, a Winnetou-type to sweep me off my feet and introduce me to a world where Father's approval is not my making or breaking. But *marriage*? The thought is almost too ridiculous to contemplate, especially at sixteen. I've decided I won't get married before eighteen, at least.

I must distract Father from the subject with an intelligent question. I search my brain.

"Father, when we came home from Sattelpeinstein with Sister Lisa, you mentioned that you had worked for the Wehrmacht near Nuremberg. What did you do there?"

I've chosen a dangerous subject, but I plunge in anyway.

Father sips his beer and avoids my gaze. "Oh, that. After they sent me home from Russia in 1943, I worked as a doctor there.

"And what did you do?"

"Administrative stuff. Paperwork."

A dead end. But now my desire to change the subject from my marriage prospects has morphed into a genuine curiosity. I need to know the extent of Father's participation with the Nazis.

"And what did you do when the war was about to end, when you knew it was lost?" My heart hammers in my chest.

Father rubs his eyes, then looks at a spot on the wall.

"There was chaos all around us. Especially in Nuremberg. Bombs fell every minute—everything was being destroyed, and people fled. They tried to escape the Russians. I had to secure files and drive them to Munich. Some other soldiers came; we drove in two Jeeps. The Jeep that was in front of me carried two officers—it exploded. Anyway, I survived and was able to secure the files." Father takes another sip of beer. "It was such a long time ago."

I imagine Father as a young man, watching helplessly as two of his comrades are blasted to bits. For a moment, I feel sympathy. Yet I still have so many questions.

"What files?"

"Administrative files. The Wehrmacht wanted them to be safe."

Although the war was lost, Father hadn't given up. He'd chosen to secure the files after narrowly escaping a bomb blast. Father must have been convinced that he was doing the right thing. Or why remain in the fight until its bitter end?

"Wow, a Jeep exploded, and you saw it." I let the sentence hang in the air in the hopes that Father will add to it.

"Everything was so tumultuous, with the war planes flying over us all of the time. It took us several days to reach Munich. So many people were on the roads, trying to escape the bombings. Sometimes the roads were gone, obliterated by the bombs."

"Who was with you?"

"One other officer." Father grows quiet, his face lined with remembrance.

"What did you do when the Jeep exploded?"

He laughs, short and bitter. "We had no time. We left the road and managed to drive around."

No time. Were the files in his Jeep more important than the fallen officers? Was carrying out orders more important than human life?

"That was the war." Father gulps the rest of his beer and leans back in his chair.

I swallow and summon my courage. Father has not lashed out at me yet; I must press on, learn what I can.

"And in Munich? What happened there?"

"I turned the files over. Soon after, I was caught by the Americans. I worked in a military hospital for them until they released me. Then I had to go to Berlin. I started work at the hospital as an assistant medical director. I worked night and day. I had a room there. There was so much to do. We had hardly any medicine, and it was my duty to help the people, to cure them."

From the way Father gazes at the wall, I can tell there is more. How often does he mention his time in the war—with whom could he share it? Does he long to be asked?

"The people in Berlin were so hungry. Many were starving. They would search in the forests for food. So many had food poisoning because they would eat entire mushrooms. We had to send out a press release telling them not to do this. We worked and worked, getting mushroom chunks out of people's stomachs."

I remember; when I was four, I ate a cigarette. My parents and their guests had been smoking. I'd watched the white sticks getting smaller and smaller and assumed the grown-ups ate them.

I was in the hospital room alone when a doctor and nurse forced me to swallow a rubber tube big as a garden hose so they could pump my stomach. I remember screaming, a nurse bringing me back to Mom, who'd complained that she'd heard me crying.

I picture Father, forcing rubber hoses down throat after throat, starving Berliner after starving Berliner.

"I had never worked so hard in my life." Father stubs out his cigarette and stands. "I'm going to watch the news now."

Father leaves me behind in the kitchen. He doesn't need to tell me to clean up—of course I will. I clear his dinner plate and the serving dish full of bread, meat, and cheese.

As I wash the dishes in the sink, I congratulate myself on switching the subject from my so-called impending marriage. I'm also glad that I got more information out of Father about the war and managed to not cross his invisible line. I never know where it is—like an enemy's encampment, it moves all the time—but I know crossing the line sends Father into a rage and may result in a beating.

But I want more. Father is hiding something—from me, maybe from himself. What did he *really* think of Hitler? His ignorance about the Holocaust—is this real, or a comforting lie which has taken on the feeling of truth after all these years?

If I knew the truth, I would understand Father better—and perhaps myself too. Until then, it is he and I, alone in a house of secrets.

26 THE BYSTANDER

"Does this look good?" Elsa raises a tennis ball.

"Yes. Very elegant."

She smashes it over the net with her forehand. I hit the ball back to Elsa, who stops it with her racket and gets into position for her backhand. "What about this? How does it look?"

She sails the ball over the net. "You look good."

They are the words Elsa wants to hear—yet I have a hard time forcing them out. She grates on my nerves with her vanity. I don't know why Elsa needs all this attention; she is already top of her class and a sports star. But it seems this is not enough for her.

Elsa has begun playing tennis daily, and I join her three or four times a week. Each day, there is less of my sister; her legs have become matchsticks and cheekbones protrude in her face. Elsa no longer eats and plays tennis for two or three hours each day. I'm surprised she can stand, never mind hold up a racket.

"What do you think about my serve?"

"It's great," I say.

Does she really need my affirmation? Is Elsa so desperate for approval that she'll take it from me, her little sister?

Even with Elsa's diminished frame, she dominates the court. We play two sets; I lose both. Afterwards we hop on our bikes and pedal the ten-minute distance to home, where we both head upstairs to take our showers. Gerda is out with the Free Christ congregation; it is only us at home.

But then the bathroom door bursts open and Father storms in on Elsa and me, each of us half-naked.

"You played *tennis*?"

Someone at the tennis club must have seen us and told Father. His gaze is trained on Elsa, his face mottled with rage. He is slightly out of breath from storming up the stairs.

Elsa says nothing.

"How many times have I told you that you are not allowed to play *tennis*? To do *any* sports?"

Has Father said this to my sister? I think he did once, last week. It was such a random instruction I hadn't paid much attention to it—and besides, the rule was meant for Elsa.

As Father closes the door behind him, the spacious bathroom feels much too small. Father's anger engulfs the room; he raises his arm and hits Elsa with full force on her naked back.

"*Stop!*" Elsa screams and raises her fists to fight back.

"I said you are not *allowed!*" Father roars.

"Dad, stop it," I say, but his eyes are wild and raging, and I doubt he even heard me. Father turns and raises his arm as if to beat me as well, but then his big hand falls on Elsa's naked body with a clapping sound again. He pounds my sister with blow after blow; Elsa screams and raises her arms to protect her head. She manages to scramble to her feet and make a break for the bathroom door—if she goes, will Father turn his anger toward me?—but Father seizes her and shoves her back down on the stone floor. He continues beating her; he doesn't speak, doesn't scream, but his fists fall like rain, again and again.

I have asked Father to stop, and nothing has happened. I

stand, frozen, watching my almost-grown sister getting beat up. There is nothing to do but wait for Father to satisfy his rage. This is how bystanders must have felt when Jews were dragged from their homes and flogged in the streets: helpless and gripped by fear.

Elsa crawls under the sink and clutches the metal pipe—she is so shrunken that fitting in the space is not a challenge. She clings to the pipe with her face toward the back of the cabinet so Father will not be able to pull her out. It doesn't stop Father; he continues to pummel her naked back. At last, he stands, shoves fallen strands of hair from his red face, and leaves the room, out of breath from hitting my sister. I kneel and approach her huddled frame, Elsa's bony and moon-white back now covered in red welts. I was not able to keep her safe.

I was not able to keep her safe.

Elsa never once cries. She has remembered Father's rule against crying from our many years of his abuse. It is so quiet, I can't hear Elsa breathe.

"Can I help you?" It is such a weak, stupid question, but I don't know what else to ask.

"No, you can't. Go away." Then after a moment, "I'm okay."

She stares at the gray-tiled wall, her gaze empty. It is obvious my sister doesn't want me here. All I can do is leave.

All I can do is leave.

Later in my room, I lie on my bed and wonder at what has happened to Elsa. She plays tennis manically to lose more weight. She keeps up a careful ruse; Elsa's bedroom is stocked with chips, peanuts, and other unhealthy snacks which she stashes behind her bed. I'd entered her room the other day and seen all the brightly colored aluminum bags.

"Do you want some?" Elsa spread out her treasure trove on the bed.

I wanted it, rabidly. But I shook my head. "I don't want to gain weight."

"But you're so thin," Elsa giggled.

I gaped at my sister, confused. Did she really believe this? If so, what did Elsa see when *she* looked in the mirror? She was skin and bones, and yet the manic tennis-playing continued.

"Here; eat this." Elsa extended a bag of red peanut flips to me—my favorite. When I didn't reach for the bag, Elsa said, "I've already eaten two bags today; I'm not hungry. You take them."

Greedily, I ate them all.

Later, Gerda confided in me,

"You know, she doesn't eat any of those snacks she has behind her bed."

"She doesn't?"

Gerda shook her head. "She wants us to *think* she eats. But she's never opened a single bag. The anorexia is making her a liar."

Elsa has become a liar and an anorexic and the object of Dad's rage—she who I used to believe was his favorite, who I always looked up to. And I had been unable to stop any of it. Even worse, I had been so absorbed in my own world I didn't even know what was happening.

I roll over on my bed, heaviness invading my whole body. It is useless to think I would have stood up for the Jews in my community and stopped the Nazis, that had I been alive during the Holocaust, I would have risked it all and done the right thing.

I can't even stand up to one person and protect those most dear to me.

27 ON MY OWN

It seems as if my sisters seek any means of escape from our house. Elsa disappears before our eyes, day by day. One day I come home from school, and Rahni tells me she is in the hospital for her eating disorder. I feel relieved that she is getting help, even though my worry for her remains. No one can match Elsa's will. Will the doctors and nurses be successful in forcing food down her throat? I remember the Baader-Meinhof group, the forced feedings they had endured in prison, and shiver. I hope it will not be like that for my sister.

Meanwhile, Gerda disappears to her room. We no longer walk to school together; I meet with my friend Gabi, and we cover the five kilometers on our bikes. At home, Gerda retreats to her bed; I find her there more and more often. One afternoon, I enter and the heavy stench of alcohol—that I know all too well from Father's bedroom—hangs in the air.

I glance out the window; summer is approaching. The lilac bushes will bloom soon, and the trees are full of cherry blossoms. I remember Hans and me playing hide and seek in the yard when we were children. The memory feels like it's from another lifetime.

It is the perfect day to be outside, yet Gerda has barricaded herself under the blankets of her bed. A half-empty bottle of wine sits by her bedside. I am shocked. Is there something I can do to help her?

"How are you?" I speak the words tentatively. Lately the slightest little thing can send Gerda into despair. "Where did you get the bottle of wine?"

"From the wine cellar." Gerda's voice is muffled by the sheets. "I don't want to talk about it."

"Have you heard from Elsa at the hospital?"

"No. I don't want to talk to her; she only lies."

I'm surprised by Gerda's harsh words.

"Can I help you with anything?" My words sound pathetic —I don't know what I could possibly help Gerda with. The loneliness that has grown inside me since Mom left fills the room.

"School is depressing me too much," Gerda says into her pillow. "Everything is depressing. I miss Mom, and Dad is making me want to explode."

Is she crying?

"Anyway, I don't know what to say." Gerda shakes her head, swallows a sob. "Ms. Koch is coming over tomorrow to talk to me. Be sure you're not around when she comes."

Ms. Koch is my biology teacher and the school drug counselor. If she's making a home visit, things must be serious with Gerda—more serious than I know.

Sure enough, next afternoon Ms. Koch rings our doorbell. She greets me with a smile, then heads upstairs to Gerda's room, brisk and determined like always. I like Ms. Koch, even though most of my classmates think she is too strict. I hope something she says will help Gerda.

I figure now is as good a time as any to visit Elsa, so I bike over to the hospital. I find my sister in a private bedroom. She looks impossibly thin and small in the metal hospital bed. A picture of Aunt Siegrid days before she died enters my mind; I shake it away.

Elsa's bare arms rest on top of the bedspread, and I see the blue marks on her right arm; bruises from Father. Has he visited her? I don't even know.

When Elsa becomes aware of me, her face doesn't change. I can't tell if she is happy to see me or not, but this is the way with our family. Our faces betray no love for each other, even if we feel it inside. On her nightstand sits a chocolate cream cake, untouched. I sit in a chair next to her bed.

"How are you?" The same question I'd asked Gerda, cowering under the covers—and a stupid one, but I don't know how else to start.

"Look, I have to eat this damn chocolate cake."

I glance to the cake. "Can I try it?" That's probably against the rules, but I want to cheer Elsa up any way I can.

"If you do, and they find out, I'll get in trouble."

"Are the people here nice?"

Elsa shrugs. "I have a nice sister nurse who's watching me. Her name is Sister Brigitte. We talk about God a lot."

As stupid as it sounds, I envy her. *I* want an older woman with whom I can talk about God, the important things.

"I can go home when I've gained some weight," Elsa adds.

"Do you want to go home?"

The question pops out of my mouth and surprises me. *Of course* a person in a hospital would want to come home. Why wouldn't they?

Yet I make an involuntary glance to Elsa's bruised arm, and she sees me. We both remembering the beating from Father, her clutching the metal pipe under the sink to shield himself from his blows. Here there is no raging Father. There is a soft bed and chocolate cake and an older nun who cares for her and tells her about God.

"Ha!" Elsa laughs, bitterly, and I understand.

Life continues in this way; Gerda in her room, drinking. Elsa—once she is released from the hospital—playing nonstop tennis. If I don't have a cello or tennis lesson, I come home from school and enter Father's study. Then I turn on his TV and watch show after show, careful to keep one ear on the entrance door for the turning of his key in the lock. When it is close to Father's coming-home time, I retreat to my room and do my homework. I change the position of my cello to make it look like I have practiced.

Most of the time, I am alone. I am used to my solitariness, though it is harder to bear when summer turns to fall and the days turn dark early. I'm happy when my sisters come home from the Free Christ church or from seeing their friends, though it isn't long before everyone retreats into their own quadrants of the house. Sometimes I see Gabi in the afternoons, but she recently got a boyfriend and is so in love with him that I avoid her more and more often, for fear of being the third wheel. In truth, her relationship fills me with longing. Why can't I have that?

Although I don't have a relationship, I have plenty of crushes on boys at school. When I screw up enough courage, I flip through the phone book for the numbers of boys in my class. The ringing of the phone on the other end of the line makes my breath catch in my throat. Each time, I hope that *this time* I'll be blessed with something witty and flirtatious to say—magic words that will make the boy holding the phone fall in love with me right there. That is never what happens.

Briiing! After several excruciating minutes, I am finally on the phone with a male classmate.

"Hi. It's Anne." Pause. Heat floods my cheeks, and my mouth goes dry. "Did you do the math homework yet?"

"No."

"Oh, okay, me neither." More terrible silence. "Did you have a good day at school?"

"It was okay."

"Good." I wait for the magic flirtatious words to be delivered, but they never come.

"Okay, well, see you tomorrow."

Click.

I replace the receiver on Father's nightstand and head back to my room, Rapunzel returning to her tower. Even though I wish for friendship and love and companionship, I am used to being alone. I can't help but wonder if this is how it will always be. The thought makes me so unbearably sad I lose my breath.

Just like my sisters, I need to find my own means of escape.

28 SATAN WILL GET YOU

Once again, I try church to see if it will give me the love I crave.

Elsa has found her own Christian community through Sister Brigitte, separate from Gerda's Free Christ congregation. One day, I accompany her to a meeting in the park in the hopes that I'll find a place there, but I'm disappointed again. The people in Elsa's church are so enthusiastic; they are convinced that God has chosen *them*. How can they be so sure? And What about everybody else?

Besides, the congregants look pale and uninteresting to me, just like the ones in Gerda's church. I have snarky, superior thoughts—*if this is what being chosen by God looks like, I don't want it*. But despite my suspicions, I feel self-conscious around the group. I wear my new jeans and yellow sweater to the park, two pieces of clothing that I love, and I top the outfit off with my golden necklace. I am the most dressed-up person here and wish I'd chosen something drab. Surely the congregants think I'm too flashy, not focused on the right things.

But my sisters' belief fills me with longing. I want that for myself. One day in their bedroom, I tell them about my old fantasy about my friend and hero Jesus, all the adventures we went on together.

Elsa and Gerda exchange a look, then turn to me with sad eyes.

"That is a fairy tale, Anne," Gerda says.

"That is not what true faith is like," Elsa adds. "When you really know God, it is different. You know without a doubt that God is with you. That's what it means to be illuminated by him."

Illuminated by God. It sounds magical.

"How do I get illuminated?"

Gerda taps the Bible in her lap. "You just have to pray, read the Bible, and think about God," she says, as if it is as simple as tying your shoes. "You'll feel it. Just be open to God. He'll accept you as you are."

Pray, read the Bible, and think about God. I can do that. I'd so enjoyed reading my children's Bible when I was younger —the stories about Noah and the ark, Moses leading his people out of Egypt, and Jacob and Esau. I love to read, anyway—if reading the Bible is my ticket, then surely illumination is near.

Each afternoon, I lock myself in my room and read the Bible as if preparing for a test. Then I pray:

"God, I love you. Please illuminate me."

Nothing.

Nothing.

Sometimes at night, I steal to Gerda's bed and snuggle with her under the covers. "Can you tell me more about how I can be illuminated?"

"Just pray and it will come," she murmurs, half-asleep.

But soon I learn there are other forces at work that may be preventing my desire for illumination. Evil forces.

One weekend, Elsa returns from a visit to the Black Forest with Sister Brigitte. Her face is full and animated—she has put on weight and looks healthier each day, thank God. While eating a bag of chips, she says,

"You know, the people in the Black Forest believe in trolls and ghosts."

"*What?*"

Elsa nods, smirking. "Yep. Brigitte even swore that she's *seen* them. The trolls and ghosts, I mean. They're small devils. The *real* devil likes to hide in the Black Forest too, because it's so dark, and he can shield himself from the sun under the tree branches. We prayed a lot to make sure the trolls didn't invade Brigitte's vacation house." Elsa pops a chip into her mouth. "It was pretty scary."

Sister Brigitte believing in trolls and devils and ghosts makes them seem real, as if they stand unseen in the bedroom. "Are the trolls sent by the devil?" I ask, my voice quaking.

"Yes. The devil can take many forms."

Something in Elsa's expression gives me pause. Is she simply pulling my leg—seeing how much nonsense her little sister will still believe?

"If there are *actual* trolls and devils, then why aren't there any stories about them on the radio or TV?"

Elsa rolls her eyes. "It's a secret, obviously. Only people who believe in God are safe. And if they don't, the devil will take them, and they'll go to hell."

Now I *absolutely* need a sign from God. I need to know that He loves me, I am illuminated, and I won't go to hell one day.

That night I am so distressed in my prayer time that I sweat. I cannot take the uncertainty—after several hours alone in my bed, I steal to Gerda's bed. Gently, I shake her awake.

"Gerda, I'm sorry. You have to tell me again. How does it feel when you get illuminated? I want to make sure I don't miss it."

Gerda rolls over and says to the ceiling, "You will feel it and just know. Once it happens, you won't doubt."

One afternoon in late fall, I sit in my room and try to do my homework. Loneliness surrounds me as twilight creeps through the window. The darkness reminds me of waking from my childhood nightmares of the men in my room. I shiver and turn on my desk lamp; I must try to keep the dark at bay.

Elsa and Gerda are out with their separate church communities, and Father is at a Philarmonic concert with a woman he met at the tennis club. Alone, thoughts of the devil obsess me. I feel foolish. Surely I am too old to be so afraid. But I can't shake my nagging thoughts.

What had Elsa said? That people who don't believe could become the devil's victims and get dragged to hell. Did that mean a troll or devil could appear in person and take me?

I haven't been illuminated, but I believe in God. Do I believe enough? Could the devil get me?

"Dear God, please illuminate me. Don't give the devil a chance to get me."

Out of nowhere, I remember the Kinder Joy egg, my eight-year-old theft. Did God still hold that against me?

"God, please forgive me for stealing. I will never do it again."

I hear something in the house. Who—or what—could it be?

I tiptoe out of my room and lean over the rail, survey downstairs from the top-floor landing. I look down into the lonely house and listen so hard for any sound my ear feels the strain. First floor: the living room, library, kitchen, cellar, bedrooms, and Father's study—all empty. I imagine unseen demons crawling about, thirsty for my soul.

I spin on my heels and race back to my room, gently closing the door behind me so I won't draw the trolls' attention. I kneel on the green carpet, grab my Bible, open it, and search for any messages of hope and comfort. Even though I'm not illuminated, the Bible can shield me from Satan—I hope. I gaze at the words, not daring to look up, lest I find myself surrounded by trolls with horns and mean, yellow eyes, their raised claws ready to tear me to shreds and drag my soul to hell.

"Don't let the devil take me, God!" I cry, tears rolling down my cheeks. "Don't let him

get me!" My whole body is bathed in sweat.

"Anne? Are you there?"

This time I am not imagining it—I *do* hear something. Gerda calls from downstairs; I hear the entrance door close behind her.

"Yes," I answer. "I'm in my room." On trembling legs, I stand and head down the stairs to Gerda.

"Is everything okay?"

I can't help it—I burst into tears and fall in my sister's arms. "I thought the devil would come and get me. I was so frightened."

"You can sleep in my room tonight," Gerda says, softly patting my head. Relief washes over me; at least tonight, I will not be alone.

Lying in bed that night, Gerda makes a surprising statement.

"I don't believe in the devil."

I'm as shocked as if she said she doesn't believe in gravity. "You don't?"

Gerda shakes her head. "I talked to Ms. Koch about it."

Ms. Koch and Gerda have become good friends, just like Sister Brigitte and Elsa. Gerda spends many afternoons at her apartment when she is not with the Free Christ church. I am grateful to Ms. Koch for how she helps my sister—Gerda has given up alcohol—and at the same time, I envy her closeness with Gerda, just as I envy Gerda her relationship with the young nurse.

"Ms. Koch thinks people invent those creatures to frighten us," Gerda continues. "That way, they can get control over us."

Gerda yawns and turns over on her side. "Don't believe what Elsa says."

I wish that Gerda's words could erase my fear, but they don't—not completely. I can't help but feel as if a reckoning is due. For what?

The question haunts me as I drift into an uneasy sleep. What sins could demand atonement? My stealing of the Kinder Joy egg and childhood lies; Elsa's lies about food; Gerda's sneaking alcohol; my sisters' and my cruelty towards Mom; Mom's desertion; Father's cruelty. Father's past.

Six million Jews, murdered. The guilt of being German, of knowing what we had done.

If the devil were to demand payment for some sin in our household, he could have his pick.

29 ANGELA

Father's friend with whom he visited the Philharmonic soon becomes more than just a friend. Mrs. Krohn, or Angela, quickly takes the place of Lisa as Father's stand-in for Mom.

Her name is not really Angela—that is only something Father likes to call her. "Because she came into our life like an angel," Father says, smiling at Angela. She beams at him from across the living room. Her real name is Gabriela. But Father is lord of this house; he can change the names of the women in it as his whim decrees. Angela it is.

I had seen Mrs. Krohn—Angela, I am still getting used to the change—a few times before she moved in. She's come to have lunch with us, and we played tennis together. Angela is attractive—tall and slim with long legs and short blond hair. She is married, or at least *was* married. What does her husband think of Angela moving in?

"Did your husband agree to let you move in with us?" I study Angela from above my coffee mug. The question is bold, but I am fourteen and deserve some answers; I will not let

Father introduce new women into our lives with no explanation.

"My husband died four months ago." With no warning, Angela begins to cry.

Oh no. What have I done? I glance to Elsa, who snickers at my unintended rudeness. I guess she knew about the dead husband. Once again, I am the last to know everything.

"I am sorry, I am sorry." Angela apologizes for her tears.

"It's all right," I say, while I think: *how can a woman this young be a widow?* Angela looks even younger than Mom. I reach to pat Angela's arm; she enfolds my hand in hers, and I like the feeling of it.

"Thank you," says Angela. "He died at the hospital. My husband was a patient of your father's. Here. . . . " She reaches in her purse, pulls out a picture of her late husband. He stares at us from under sunglasses, white hair blowing in the wind. Angela appears to have a type: old.

Soon, my reservations about Angela are gone, and I follow her around with full-blown adoration. Where Angela goes, I go: to the grocery store, tennis club, and in the kitchen as she helps prepare meals. I laugh at her jokes, and she laughs at mine. In the evenings, Angela comes to my room and gives me back massages. For the first time in my fourteen years, I am happy at home.

"You all need so much love," Angela says one evening, kneading my neck and shoulders as she kneels behind me on the bed. "I can see that there was not much love here before."

I close my eyes and breathe a deep, happy sigh. Gerda has Mrs. Koch; Elsa has Sister Brigitte. Now, at last, I have Angela.

Father is different with Angela too. He is more approachable. He laughs with his friends and in public. Father makes Angela laugh, and when she does and her blue eyes shine, his eyes light up as well.

I enjoy the nicknames Angela gives me, like "cutie" and "little pumpkin." I don't even mind that I am in tenth grade, too old for such diminutives. When my best friend Gabi comes to visit, she feels the change in our home too; I can tell by how often she smiles for Angela, how freely she tells Angela every little detail of the school day. Before, I never wanted my friends in the house. Now I wish Gabi could come over every day to bask in Angela's warmth.

But Gabi is still obsessed with her boyfriend. When she's with me, all she mentions is when she'll see *him* again. Gabi's boyfriend has a moped. They drive proudly through the streets of Berlin, and Gabi constantly talks about their many moped adventures. I seethe with jealousy.

"Why don't you hang out with us sometime, Anne?" Gabi asks for the dozenth time.

"No thanks," I mutter quickly. "I have to do extra schoolwork to get my grades up."

The truth is that I am far too envious to be near as Gabi and her boyfriend kiss and touch and giggle with each other. Perhaps that is why Gabi has begun to spend time with other friends at school, shopping with classmates at the Tauentziehen or Schlossstraße. I thought those were *our* special places. I interpret Gabi visiting with other girls to mean one thing: she doesn't want me for a friend anymore. One day after school, I confront her about it.

"I saw you with Heike and Claudia yesterday." I stare at Gabi, accusing. I let the sentence hang in the air, hoping Gabi will provide some sort of explanation.

"Yes, we went shopping."

Gabi and I head to the bike racks. I stiffen, turn my nose up in the air. There it is. Gabi has all but said that she doesn't want to be my friend anymore. I quicken my stride toward the bikes.

"What's wrong with you?" Gabi jogs to catch up.

"Nothing." I keep walking.

"You have to talk to me." Gabi falls behind me on the sidewalk.

In my mind, I've decided: the friendship is finished. I don't want to feel the pain of watching Gabi with other girls. I keep toward my bike and don't look back.

"Anne, please! Tell me why you're so upset."

In her voice, I hear suppressed tears, and this fills me with triumph. I have won. I free my bike and pedal home, alone. Ignoring Gabi has given me a high: I am powerful. I don't need her. I have Angela, and that is enough.

I am used to locking up my heart. I have locked it away from Mom, from Sister Lisa; it is easy to lock it away from Gabi too. Gabi yells after me as I pedal away, making a fool of herself in front of our classmates. She must be really upset.

Back at home, the thought makes me smirk.

Locking away my heart comes with a price—the price of meanness, aloneness. I wonder how Rapunzel could survive the loneliness of her tower. But like her, I will take it. If I lock my heart up, I'm the only one who can break it.

30 FIGHTING FOR LOVE

One day in January, the doorbell rings. Father is at the hospital, Angela is not home, and Gerda is still at school.

"I'll get it," I call to Elsa, who is somewhere in the house. I think our visitor must be one of Elsa's tennis friends or Sister Brigitte. I am totally unprepared to open the door and see Mom standing on the landing, her wry smile set in a face that's too pale.

"Hello," she says.

I survey her black clothes against the gray back drop of our front yard in winter. It looks as if Mom is in mourning.

"May I come in?"

I step aside and make room for her to enter our house again. It has been one year since she's left our home.

I'm unsure where to go. If we stay in the living room, Elsa may come out and make a scene. I climb the stairs toward my bedroom, and Mom follows, then takes a seat in my white armchair. She looks so fragile in it. Has she grown smaller, or have I grown bigger? She's never sat in this chair before, I realize.

"How are you?" Mom asks.

What a pathetic question. There is no way to catch up Mom on the last year of my life: my attempts to flirt with boys, my separation from Gabi, my burning desire to be illuminated, my deep loneliness, and Angela. Angela who has made it all bearable, just barely.

"I am okay." I try not to sound too okay. Mom left; she will always have to pay for that. I won't give her the satisfaction of letting her believe she did the right thing.

One year of unspoken truths hang in the space between us. We sit on either side of the room, the air thick with tension. My breaths come shallow and short; I feel ready to burst.

Mom bursts first.

"You know, I had to go and leave you." Mom's words rush out. "I was going to kill myself."

How do I answer this? I am shocked; Mom and I share something. A year ago—before she left—our house was so infected with bitterness and rage and cruelty that I thought about killing myself too. Why hadn't we been able to talk about it?

"You were?"

"Yes, Anne. Dad didn't want me to work here in Berlin. I was dying inside, a prisoner to this house. I wanted to do so much more." She straightens. "But the law changed. I didn't need his permission to work anymore. What I needed was freedom—freedom to live my own life." Mom looks at her hands in her lap. "How is it now? At home?"

Now I *really* don't know how to answer. The truth: things are much better with Angela in our home than they had ever been with Mom. There is love and warmth and laughter for the first time that I can remember. But I don't want to add to Mom's pain by telling her that.

"Everything is all right. Angela is looking after us. It's okay."

Mom smiles, even though her eyes look pained. "I'm glad. I'm going to go see the rest of the house...."

She stands, looks around my room—lost for a moment—before heading toward the door. She is a stranger in her own home.

I wait until Mom's footsteps have receded down the stairs, then follow her to the top of the landing. The door to Elsa's room opens and closes. Soon, there are screams coming from behind it.

"It is so much better here without you!" Elsa shouts.

"This is because of Mrs. Krohn," Mom shouts back. "She and Dad have poisoned your mind against me. I can't believe he let her in this house—just weeks after I left!"

"We never learned *anything* from you or Dad," screams Elsa. "We didn't know what it is like to be liked by someone. You always *hated* us. Angela is different."

Oh God. Has Elsa finally gone too far? Mom had wanted to kill herself before. Will Elsa's words drive her to it now?

Elsa's door slams and Mom storms from the room down to the entrance door. She puts on her boots and flies out the front door. Elsa and Mom's screams echo throughout the now-silent house; the storm has come and gone, quick as a tornado. I stand at the top of the stairs, unsure what to do. Do I go to Elsa or run after Mom?

At long last, I pad down the stairs and gently push open Elsa's door. I'm shocked to find my sister sitting on the edge of her bed, her face resolute.

"Maybe I shouldn't have said that," Elsa mutters. "But that is how I feel."

"She will not be angry for long," I say, even though I don't know if it's true. Will Mom forgive Elsa? Does she plan to stay in Berlin, and if so, will Angela leave? God, I don't want that. But I don't want Mom to disappear again either.

I go to Elsa's side, pat her on the back, and wonder what on earth will happen next.

The downstairs doorbell rings again.

Elsa runs down and opens the door. Footsteps pound furiously up the stairs, and I flee to my room, frightened. Then, I am four again, and Mom is chasing me with a hanger. I hear slamming doors from the direction of the bathroom. Adrenaline pumps through me; I jump to my feet and follow the noise. *Crack.* Something shatters on the porcelain tile.

Above the sink is a shelf with all of Angela's cosmetics: cleansing milk, perfume, and makeup bottles. With one fell swoop, Mom sweeps her arm across the shelf and smashes the products onto the floor. Then she slams open the cabinet next to the sink in a desperate search for more of Angela's things. Mom plucks them one by one and hurls them onto the tile. Shampoo: *crack.* Moisturizer: *crack.* Lipstick: *crack.*

"I hate her!" Mom screams wild as a banshee. "This is a disgrace!" Another item hurtles to the floor. "*I hate her!*"

At last, Mom is spent. She sobs into the crook of her arm, wails echoing throughout the bathroom. Has she forgotten I'm here? Should I go to her, hold out my arms and enfold her, and tell her what I do not believe myself: that everything will be all right?

The powder from Angela's blush and eye shadow covers the floor like a layer of dirt. A puddle of cleansing milk pools around my feet like spilled blood.

Mom walks by me and out the door, still sobbing into her arm. I have no way to reach her in her grief, no way to know where to begin. She leaves the house as quickly as she came.

I do what I do in the wake of chaos: fetch a mop and try to clean the mess before Angela comes home.

31 SHE IS GONE II

After another year, everything is over. In May 1982, Angela leaves, too. I am fifteen. The wonderful dream bursts like a pricked balloon.

I stand with her at the back door as she hugs me tight and says through tears. "I am sorry. You girls deserve so much love." The previous Saturday, she'd broken the news that she would soon be moving out. I don't blame her.

Angela is moving back to her old apartment on the other side of West Berlin. Gerda is leaving within the next few weeks as well.

Angela: the tall pretty woman with the short blond hair who came to us strong, vibrant, and laughing. But this house—Father—has killed something inside of her. She leaves us smaller than the woman who came.

In the previous weeks, a cold war had formed between Angela and Gerda and Elsa and Father. Elsa and Father's alliance has coalesced and become even more sinister. Elsa spewed hate toward Angela at all hours of the day and claimed that she would leave, that she couldn't bear the woman Dad wanted to marry. This is how Elsa secures Father's love: by destroying all competitors, no matter how badly he has treated her.

Elsa and Father versus Gerda and Angela—and where am I?

Since Mom's smashing of the makeup bottles one year ago, Angela has changed. The broken shards of her belongings that I had tried to clean up so carefully; those fragments had cut her heart. Her pain had grown, conquered her good intentions and her love. She was not tough enough to overlook mom's eruption and Elsa's growing meanness towards her. Instead, she weakened, shrunk. Angela stopped eating, just as Elsa did before her; we watched her shrink before our eyes. It was Gerda who saved her. In that atmosphere, there was no room anymore for love, it was suffocated by jealousy.

These last few months I've sequestered myself in my room, feeling like a bomb has gone off in our home. Angela was fading away, so I had fallen back upon my old trick of locking up my heart. I stopped talking to Angela. At first, I felt good about it. I was a part of her sadness; I refused to be her "pumpkin" or "cutie" anymore. Now, watching her leave, I feel only misery. If I had been different, would she have stayed?

I cannot count on Angela, just as I cannot count on Mother, Father, Elsa, or Gerda. One way or another, everyone leaves. Long ago, I mastered the art of building walls. I laid bricks around my heart when Mom sent me to my room and forced me to endure my nightmares alone, when Father and Mother gave me the punishment of long confinements for some small infraction. The walls around my heart remain.

Since Angela has left, Father and Elsa wait in the living room for Gerda to come home every night. Gerda will leave soon and has found an apartment near Angela. I can see that she has toughened up. While helping Angela to leave, *she* became strong. Her strength enables her to stand up to Father and Elsa. Meanwhile, I cannot sleep anymore because of the tension in this house.

When Gerda comes home, she must answer to Father and Elsa's inquiries: "Where were you?" Elsa demands.

"Your grades are so bad; how will you graduate from high school if you continue like that?" Father shouts, his voice the threatening tone I know so well. Although I stand behind Gerda in my nightgown, observing the scene and wanting to protect her, I am invisible to them.

One night Gerda calls social services and claims that she feels threatened by my sister and father. A caseworker arrives at our house, questioning Father about the status of his relationship to us. Father grows agitated around her, his carefully cultivated urbane demeanor cracking.

"Everyone goes crazy here," Father mutters when she is gone. "There are only crazy women around me. They do what they want and make me look bad."

It is always the woman's fault for not loving enough. As if love could survive within these four walls.

With each passing day, I see him more clearly. Rejection from the woman he wanted to marry weighs on him. He listens to Wagner, The Ring Cycle—I believe the music, bombastic and dazzling, is an expression of the feelings that he cannot express. He blasts it to drown out his numbness. Father escapes into this music, and the exhilaration takes him away. But naturally, the crash comes; what goes up must go down. All of Father's money and control and prestige cannot make up for the loneliness of his soul; the love he never received from *his* father who fell for his country in WWI, the love he hardened his heart against. Without this love there is fear. War. The need for certainty, rightness. The Second World War may have ended decades ago, but for Father it is never over. The two wars rage in his heart.

And they rage in mine too.

It is as it's always been.

I think about Rapunzel and how she must have felt when the witch cut off her wonderful hair. I imagine the witch taking big scissors, laughing at Rapunzel while she cries, hurting her on purpose. In that moment, Rapunzel must have felt like she wanted to die.

I fall back on my bed. Mom's words from one year ago float back to me. *I was going to kill myself, Anne.*

I close my eyes, and the words call me like a siren song. I wish to close them forever.

Throughout the coming weeks, the thought of killing myself grows and grows.

In Father's nightstand, there are sleeping pills. I've sat in front of that nightstand many times, during my excruciating phone calls with boys that go nowhere. Opening and closing the nightstand calms my nerves; it is filled with English toffees, various vitamin bottles, nasal sprays, and the pills. The small round jar of Valiums gets refilled regularly. One afternoon I take one pill—just one—and hide it beneath my pillow to see what will happen.

Nothing. Father has not noticed the theft.

Over the next couple of weeks, a plan forms in my head. Finally, I have a way out; Angela has left, and so will I. The plan uplifts me. There is an end to my suffering.

A few days later, I stare into the bathroom mirror, the same bathroom where Mom had destroyed Angela's cosmetics and Elsa hid underneath the sink as Father beat her. The sink is sparkling white, cleaned by Rahni. Father had left it with bits of toothpaste and shaving cream that morning—but of course, there is always a woman around to clean up his mess.

It is 10:00 a.m. The big house is empty. I don't go to school; I give the excuse that the teacher is sick and class has been canceled.

I smile at the thought of finally being with Jesus. Soon he and I will be together; I will look down on my family. They probably will not miss me; at last, I will be freed from my sadness.

I swallow the first pill.

Then, there are doubts. Does this Jesus really exist? Is he just a girlhood fantasy, formed by too much TV-watching and meshed with my fantasies of America and Winnetou and romance? Killing yourself is a mortal sin; that is what our children's pastor always says. I could end up in hell. I recall Elsa's warnings about the devil roaming the Black Forest, his minions who can appear at any time and spirit souls away. "God is eternal happiness; Satan is eternal loneliness," Elsa has said. I have had enough loneliness for one lifetime. I cannot endure it for all of eternity.

"God, please forgive me," I plead again, another pill working its way down my throat.

I swallow more pills, quickly, before I can change my mind. Whatever will happen will happen. I remember the evening I had been so terrified Satan would appear and drag me to hell —the old fear comes back and grips every cell in my body. My last thought is that I wish I could undo it: vomit all the sleeping pills and leave Father's bathroom, undo the eternal thing that I've done. I try to gag myself so that the pills will come back up —but in vain. Leaden gravity fills my body, and as my strength slips away, I go to my bedroom and fall on the bed sobbing.

Then I slip into darkness.

32 FREEING RAPUNZEL

When I blink my eyes open, Father shakes my arm. I am not in heaven or hell; I am right here where I've always been. I don't know how long Father has been here in my room, this fortress no one enters but me.

"Anne." He looks at me, appraising. Does he know what I've done? "I have tickets for the Haydn Cello Concert. You come with me. Hurry, it starts soon."

I am still drowsy from the pills, but I have to make believe that I only took a nap.

"Just a second." I murmur and clench my teeth to fight the fatigue.

I can never tell Father about the pills. He will treat me as defective, "mentally disturbed," send me to a hospital, and make me talk to someone. It would be like when he sent Elsa to the hospital for her anorexia.

"Put that on. And that." Out of my closet, he pulls a navy-blue skirt and a white blouse. Never in my life has Father taken such care with me. His back is to me, so he misses the ridiculous view of me getting up. Now I know how a drunk must feel after downing a dozen bottles of liquor. Under no circumstances will I allow myself to fall asleep again.

On the drive to the symphony, I feel Father's eyes inspect me from time to time. If he suspects what I have done, he will never say it, just like I have made a vow of secrecy. I struggle to keep my eyes open. I am so relieved when we arrive and find our seats in the audience; we can look straight ahead, and I can pretend I am invisible right next to Father.

Then the music starts: the Haydn Cello concert, the one I am studying right now in my cello lessons. It is unbearably beautiful. Despite my otherworldly tiredness, something kindles in me. A small light of happiness. Is it the music I know so well that lets me feel hopeful, even light?

Father's elbow digs into my side. I must have fallen asleep.

"Anne," he demands, "concentrate."

I blink my eyes back open. Despite my fatigue, the feeling of lightness stays. Later, after the concert, I stagger to my room and fall asleep within an instant. This time my sleep is restful and carries with it the hope of a new tomorrow.

When I wake up the next day, the lightness remains, like I've taken off a heavy coat that almost suffocated me. I am alive. Today is a new day.

For so long, I have been paralyzed, watching other people live their lives. Elsa, Gerda, Gabi—they've stepped out, found new communities, fought bitterly, tried, failed, and tried again. Mom left. Angela left. The people in my world have caused me great pain with their choices, but they've made choices, as I've sat like a mole in my room, waiting for something to happen.

Something has happened. My room—the same as it has always been—looks different. Brighter. Light streams through the window and makes dancing shadows on the fir tree patterned wallpaper.

The light illuminates a truth I can finally see clearly: Father is a despot. As long as he has charge of this house, I cannot have a true place in it. Nothing will ever change. Father's beating of me after I stole the Kinder Joy egg; the hours-long hikes he made us endure in the rain; his cruelty toward Mom; Father's raging, his beating of Elsa and Gerda. Mom could not change him. Angela could not change him, and neither could social services. Now I straddle two worlds, Father and Elsa on one side and Angela and Gerda on the other. But I cannot always be in the middle.

I must free myself.

As I put on my clothes, disjointed pieces of my life fall into place, arrange in a pattern. Any woman who falls into Father's realm suffers, including me. God knows Father has suffered. I will never know what he witnessed in those battles in Russia, what living horrors fill his dreams. But I do know this; those nightmares have transferred into my soul. They keep me in chains.

I survey my room, my closest ally all these years. Here I have played the part of Rapunzel for so long. Even the things we love can become a prison. While Gerda, Mom, and Angela have sought a better life outside of this house, I have holed up within these four walls as if they could protect me from pain. But the pain was always *inside*—Father's legacy to us all. My room cannot protect me.

It is time for Rapunzel to climb down from her tower. I have left the job of rescuing me to a man who doesn't exist. Perhaps he will come into form, someday. But for now, I can wait no longer.

I have left the job of rescuing me to a man who doesn't exist. Perhaps he will come into form, someday. But for now, I can wait no longer.

Once again, I am a little girl with Aunt Anna. She sits on the edge of the bed and reads me the story of Rapunzel. How does it end?

After her discovery of Rapunzel's prince, the witch cut her

hair and cast her into the wilderness to fend for herself. Then, using the long rope of hair and a false voice, the witch tricked the prince into climbing the tower. She threw him from the tower; the prince fell into brambles and was blinded. Rapunzel and the prince wandered, solitary, for years—until at long last they found each other. Rapunzel's tears restored sight to the prince.

I may have to wander like Rapunzel. Perhaps the years ahead will be as painful as the years in Father's home. But I cannot know unless I leave. Maybe one day, like Rapunzel, I can take my pain and transform it into something that heals. Maybe out of all this heartache will come beauty.

Leaving the tower will be difficult but not impossible. *You all need so much love,* Angela had said. I open the door to my room and step down the stairs, determined to find the love that I deserve. Somehow, I know that this love must start on the inside. I must give it to myself.

Downstairs, I step outside and breathe in the fresh air that bears fragrances of the coming spring. A wind gust ruffles the leaves, then caresses my face; I smile at its gentle touch.

It is time to begin.

33 L'SHANA HABA'AH B'YERUSHALAYIM (AUF WIEDERSEHEN IN JERUSALEM)

Five Years Later - July 1987

When we arrive in the old city of Jerusalem, I am exhausted from the long bus ride. My short hair sticks up in all directions; the intense heat nearly suffocates me the minute I climb down the bus stairs. But I pay these discomforts no mind. I am bursting with excitement to be here in this mystical, ancient town at the center of so many religious traditions.

I have graduated college and am now a certified economic correspondent in English and French. Bucking Father's plans for my future, I went to college and got a degree. My parents surprised me with this trip as a graduation present. For three weeks, fifteen young people and I will embark across Israel on a study tour organized by the Rotary Club.

After many hours of travel by plane and bus, we are now here on this tiny strip of land where so many news headlines are generated. Our tour started with a bus drive in darkness from Tel Aviv to Be'er Sheva. Since all my tour-mates are German-speaking, I hadn't worried about disguising my accent on the bus. There is a mutual understanding between us; besides wanting to discover the richness of Israel's history, we acknowledge the atrocities our people committed on the Jews; we've come here to see for ourselves what the lasting impact of that dark legacy is.

We wish to make amends, but also to feel hope. We want to see the former victims of our collective genocide flourishing, to be reminded that life does go on, to integrate the guilt we carry and learn how to turn it into goodness in the world. Perhaps we also want to prove to the Israelites: *things have changed and gotten better; we recognize the sins of our fathers and are determined not to be like them.* My travel group is made up of three Austrians—Peter, Andrea, and Karin, and three Germans—Silke, Tobias, and Johannes.

We wander the streets of the old city. I explore crowded, narrow alleyways. Exotic herbs and spices mix with tobacco; the scents fill my nose as my feet become dusty, my mouth parched. We search for a Lutheran guest house, which will serve as our base camp in Jerusalem. At last, we find it, unload our bags—but we are all too excited to rest. My group decides to find the Mount of Olives.

The faces in the crowded streets are every shade of brown. Women sit with one another on stoops and gossip; men stand in doorways, their white linen shirts untucked, laughing and gesticulating as they smoke pipes; veiled women in burkas stand together and discuss a shoe purchase from the market. I feel almost dizzy—from lack of sleep and the air's rich perfume—as I walk past them, try to take it all in. In the babble of voices, I pick out Arabic and Hebrew, but there are other languages in the mix. All these different voices funnel into a constant humming noise which reverberates off the stone walls of the ancient homes. I bathe in the sensations.

My old classmate Rebecca, Ariana's twin sister—what if I find her here? She recently moved to Israel. Amir, Gerda's former classmate, told me about it when I bumped into him at the Wiener Konditorei.

"Do you know Rebecca moved to Israel for good?"

"No, I didn't. Why?" My instinct told me to proceed carefully. I deeply respected Amir—God forbid I reveal some ignorance or prejudice and be called a Nazi. My guilt is at the forefront of every interaction I have with a Jewish person.

"She didn't like it here anymore. She thought there were still too many people who have something against Jews." Amir sipped his coffee. "Israel, though, is our country. Rebecca thought she would belong there."

Rebecca had crossed continents in the hope of finding true belonging. How brave she was.

I recall my conversation with Amir as I wander Jerusalem's crowded streets. Perhaps it was true, that there are still too many Germans who were prejudiced against Jews. I want to believe things are better. Within the last few years, the Green party has been on the rise. They are liberal, open-minded, and democratic—so different from the conservative idealogues to whom Father had given his loyalty. The conservatives had had to adapt to the fresh wind. The new political scene gave me hope. Germany was finally leaving its dark past behind, once and for all. Couldn't everyone feel it?

Not Amir. That day in the Wiener Konditorei, his jaw set, and a hardened look came over him.

"Rebecca is right. There are so many Nazis here. They all hate us."

His beautiful, soft face had become petrified in an instant. It shocked me.

"Did you know Hitler took my family's factory? After the

war, it was in such bad shape. My father took a huge financial loss trying to restore it, and he had just lost *his* parents in Auschwitz." Amir gazed out the window. "I hate it here. I hate Germany. I hate all the Christians."

I felt inept in the face of his suffering. I hated that I was partly responsible for his pain, even though I had not been born during the time of Hitler's atrocities. Amir wanted revenge, but how could that be possible? No reparation could account for his hardship. Nothing anyone could do would ever be enough to make up for what he had suffered. Time can transpose and heal a country. But for some, there will never be enough time. It had only been forty years since the war. That day in the Konditorei, I realized that healing could not be measured in decades but in centuries.

In Jerusalem, people seem to smile easily. The people are known for their jovial, easy-going nature, but something simmers under the surface. A bus was bombed earlier this month. Two Gaza students had been shot by Israeli soldiers on the campus of Birzeit University the previous December. Our group had questioned the wisdom of this trip and considered canceling due to safety concerns.

But my group walks on, basking in the warmth of the sun. At last, we reach the Mount of Olives and sit next to each other on the grass. Here it is cooler than in the old city; a breeze caresses my cheeks. I drink in the view of Jerusalem from the mountain. There are few tourists; it feels as if this mountain is here for our own pleasure, so we may revel in its history and feel connected to all the stories that have gone before us—one thread in the great tapestry of humanity.

The following day I go to the supermarket to buy some snacks. In line, a tall older woman with short blond hair pays for her items. She hands her money over and I shudder; on her wrist are engraved six numbers, almost faded but still visible. The woman meets my eyes; I stare back, unable to look away.

I have to walk past the woman outside the store. I try to catch up to my peers, but the woman says, "Are you visiting?" It is as if she's been waiting for me.

I stop in my tracks. I am not used to a stranger addressing me in the street—no one would do that in Germany. But this woman is German too; I recognize her accent instantly.

"Yes, I am visiting," I reply in English. I meet the woman's green eyes; a floppy sun hat casts shadows across her narrow face. The eyes look kind.

"I was born in Germany," she says in German. "I came here to Jerusalem as a child. How is it in Germany now?"

I'm caught speechless. I want to tell her things are better—but what about what Amirl had said? What about Rebecca, moving across the world to escape the hate she felt in her homeland?

"People have changed," I answer, tentative.

I wish for this to be true. Though I've only met a few people who were victims of Hitlerism—Michelle, Ariana, Rebecca, and Amir—I have read so many books about that time period. I've tried to learn everything about the rise of the Nazis so that I may do all I can to prevent it from happening again. I've finally understood and accepted that Father—he who was always "right"—was terribly misled; that he swallowed a lie and kept on swallowing it. Father fought for the wrong cause and lost. In his wake, there are millions of victims; he is a victim too, as well as perpetrator.

Mom, my sisters, and Angela—*we* have been victims; Father kept his pain buried deep inside, but it spilled out and threatened our lives. My father had never wanted to talk about his shame in fighting a losing war. He is no different from thousands of older Germans. Their leader—Hitler—killed himself; this compounded their shame. They, the instigators the losers, were not worth standing up for. Father has carried this sense of betrayal forward through the decades. We who shared his house have been marinated in his guilt and rage. But what does this mean in the face of a Holocaust survivor? Despite all my reading, I don't know how to answer.

"I am here with a youth group," I say. Just then, Tobias comes toward me. He has short black hair, dark eyes, and tanned skin; he could pass for an Israeli.

"Hello." Tobias greets us with a smile.

"Hello," the woman says. "Are you with her?"

Tobias nods.

The woman smiles at us with sad eyes. "I miss Germany. I hope it has changed." She sighs. "But I will never go back. Goodbye."

She turns from us and walks back to wherever she came from. Tobias and I watch her leave; I whisper to him about the marks on the woman's wrist. In my mind, I wish the woman well. I can never account for her pain, the marks she received in a concentration camp as a child. I can only hope that her present life is full of healing, joy, love, and laughter.

I hope the same for myself.

For two nights, we stay with Jewish and Palestinian families in Nazareth. I am in Upper Nazareth with a family of four. There is a mother with two sons, ages sixteen and eighteen, and a father away on a business trip. At dinner, the mother explains the kosher custom of not mixing milk with meat. We had been told this during cultural orientation, but I forgot why it was important.

"Do not cook a kid in its mother's milk," the mother says. "In Kabbalah, meat represents judgment and milk represents kindness. Those are two opposing characteristics which should not be mixed."

Judgment does not mix with kindness. I make a note to remember this fragment of the law.

In the evening, the older son offers to take me on a moped tour around town. We meet his friends at a park. They are curious to hear about my group and where some of our members are staying.

I reply hesitantly, "Some of us stay here in Upper Nazareth; some are in Nazareth."

Our group has learned about the Palestinian-Israeli conflict over land which both sides claim for themselves in old Nazareth. Now, mostly Palestinians live there. In Upper Nazareth, there is an Israeli majority.

"I hate the Palestinians."

The pronouncement comes from Joshua—my young, friendly host.

"What did you say?"

"I hate the Palestinians." He turns to face me. Joshua's friends nod their assent.

I am shocked by the strength of their pronouncement, the clear disgust I read in their faces. I try not to betray my bewilderment.

"Why do you hate them?"

"Palestinians stink. Where they live, it's filthy and dirty. Go down to Nazareth—you'll see. They pollute the water, the streets, everything."

I look into Joshua's eyes. In them is the same dangerous glint I saw in Amir's eyes in the Wiener Konditorei. How could Joshua be filled with this hate, after all that the Jewish people had endured in the recent past? Doesn't he know that hate leads nowhere?

But then I remember myself at sixteen—breaking free from the hate and prejudices Father had taught us, facing my own complicity in horror. I do not know where Joshua has heard such terrible things about the Palestinians. Maybe at home, maybe at school, perhaps everywhere. Unless someone teaches you another way—like Michelle that Sunday afternoon in my parents' living room, or Mr. Rosenstein in the Jewish Center presenting to my seventh-grade class—how can you know better?

I remember the pledge I made to myself in the Jewish Center as a seventh grader: that I will give my future firstborn child a Jewish name. Here in Upper Nazareth, seeing the scorn in Joshua's eyes, I recommit to this promise.

Perhaps it will be a small gesture, meaningless. Yet giving my child a Jewish name will signify that the cycle of hate stops with me. I will guard against prejudice in my own heart; I will not pass on ignorance and violent thoughts to the next generation. I was born into a supremacist culture, part of a heritage of genocidaires. I cannot erase what they have done. Despite my childhood fantasies of how I would have stood up for my Jewish classmates in the face of the Nazis, I can't rewind the clock.

But I can choose to love. I can love myself despite my mistakes, even though I never saw this love modeled in my family. I can love others. This love is not soft—it's a dangerous calling that will compel me to stand up in the face of injustice and do the right thing, even at great cost to myself. I get to make this choice every day, every hour, and every moment. If I choose incorrectly, I can choose again. I do not have to be a prisoner to my past—to shame—as Father has spent so many years of his life.

The memory of Joshua stays with me on the plane ride home from Tel Aviv. So does the woman from the shop with the floppy sun hat. *I will never go back.*

I will never go back, either: to ignorance, to self-hatred, to looking to others to "save me." Five years ago, when I woke up after swallowing the sleeping pills, I made the commitment to save myself. I look out the cabin window at the twinkling lights of Tel Aviv far below. I saved myself once; I will do it again, however many times are necessary.

Love will be my salvation.

34 MEDALS

Thirty Years Later, Wiesbaden 2017

I sit in the study of my sister Elsa's new home, in one of the wealthier suburban villages of Wiesbaden.

"I want to show you something," says Elsa.

Every summer I have flown across two continents and an ocean, back to Germany from my new home in Los Angeles. I have lived in America for twelve years. Call it serendipity or fate, that after all those years of being enraptured by the American fair as a child, I now live in California. My husband and I married in Germany and then made the move from one world to the other, following my husband's aspirations and business.

Father died in 2008. In his last decades, he had become a lion with soft teeth toward us sisters, though not toward mother. Father tried to keep the family together, we who were so often on the verge of breaking apart. He never repented of his past but became a tolerant person. On his deathbed, he told me how proud he was of all I'd achieved in my life. Father and I made our peace. I could forgive him. As a child, I asked myself what forgiveness felt like. Today I know that it is a relief, a lightness in my heart. To heal, it is essential to forgive others and especially ourselves.

I appreciated his belief in me and what he taught me. His death was bittersweet. After his death, mom sold the old three-story villa that had been my home for so long and moved into an apartment nearby. She died four years ago at age seventy-six due to a tragic accident. My sisters and I were in Berlin to clean out Mom's apartment and put it on the market. Now Elsa, Gerda, and I are the only remaining members of our original family unit.

On that fateful visit to clean out Mom's things, I had confirmed what I had long suspected: that Father wished me to be a boy. An heir. I found letters from my parents' friends, dated shortly after my birth in 1966. Surely after the "initial shock," my mother and father would find joy in another girl, the letters said. "We wish that after the first small disappointment, joy will predominate." Another note to Father read: "May you soon be happy and confident again after this difficult time."

Disappointment, difficult: the words that had greeted my birth. Seeing them printed on the page brought a strange relief. The picture was clear.

It was not without trepidation that I followed Elsa's invitation to her new home in Wiesbaden on this trip. Things have been rocky between us since I left for the United States. On the day of my departure, she had yelled at me over the phone: "I wish you all the bad luck in the world."

At Mom's funeral four years ago, she behaved erratically at the mourning gathering, trash talking Mom to our family members and expressing how much she had suffered under her: "She never loved us!" Two days later, she had loaded her Audi with as many of Mom's belongings as would fit inside and yelled to Gerda and me before speeding off: "I don't want to see you ever again! It's over between us." Elsa and I have not yet healed the past, have not ushered in a new adult relationship separate from the divisive connection we formed under Father's roof, but this meeting is a first step.

Yet while I've been on a healing journey in the States, Elsa has been on a healing journey too. She has delved into the past to gain a clearer picture of Father and how his many secrets affected our family. Elsa, Father's protégé; I had always believed her to be his favorite. She has followed in his footsteps and is now a prominent doctor, married to an oncologist. He is Elsa's third husband; they each brought two children into the marriage and have all the outward trappings of success. But as we understand from growing up in Father's house, outward appearances are not everything. Elsa bears her own wounds from our difficult childhood. We are only beginning to discuss it.

After we all had dinner together on the terrace facing her flowery backyard, Elsa and I withdraw ourselves into her spacious living room. Elsa opens one of the cabinets and comes back carrying a small plate bearing two medals and some silver coins. She places it on the desk in front of me.

"I found this in the attic of our parents' house. When we helped Mom move out."

I stare at the medals. One is engraved with a metal iron cross and the year 1939. Two crossed swords form an "X" in the background; it hangs on a striped red and yellow band. The other medal looks like a badge; it bears a topographical imprint of Crimea. The oversized claws of the imperial eagle rest on the swastika. The years designated on the badge: 1941 and 1942.

The sight of the swastika sends a chill through me. Here it is before me: living proof of Father's suppressed past. How did Father earn these medals? His answers to my questions about the war had always been so evasive, so unsatisfactory. He was merely a troop doctor of the Wehrmacht, a lowly sergeant who cared for the colds, stomachaches, and blisters of his comrades —or so he said. Father worked behind the scenes of the battlefield; I'd always imagined him in a white tent, away from the killing. He had been especially vague when I'd asked about his time in Russia.

"He got this one . . . " Elsa says and holds up the medal with the crossed swords, "for a fight in France, in June 1939. The troops had to cross the Somme river." Elsa walks to the kitchen; she plucks a wineglass from the cabinet, fills it with merlot, and brings it to me.

If Father was involved in the fighting in France, did he kill people? I take a sip of wine. "How do you know this?"

"I asked Uncle Theo. Father confided in him when he came back from the war. Theo was too young to fight, but he was so proud of Dad. Theo believes Dad must have been in the first boat which crossed the Somme."

I had loved Uncle Theo, Father's cousin from Nuremberg. I'm glad Elsa mined his memory for answers—Theo has been dead one year. The giants from our past are slipping beyond us.

Elsa leans forward. "I believe Father was heavily involved in the fighting, that he killed. He was not the harmless troop doctor he painted himself as."

After Mom's death, Gerda had discovered a small gray diary kept by Father during the war years. The lined paper had yellowed with age. Father kept the diary for fourteen days and then stopped. I had pored over Father's small, neat handwriting, a mixture between Sütterlin script—the old German handwriting taught in schools from 1915 to 1941—and his familiar cursive. Why had he stopped writing? When the fighting commenced, did he put down his pen?

Now I recall one sentence that caught my attention in his diary: "But now it is time for revenge!" Written on the day of

Belgium's capitulation to Germany—Belgium, where my grandfather had fallen near Ypres.

Ghosts of the past surround me: Father and Uncle Theo, my grandfather who had fallen in the First World War. The huge house seems to fill with their echoes. From the basement, I hear my two sons, Ariel and Tim, playing ping pong with Elsa's daughter. Their teenage voices comfort me; they bring me back to the present.

"Remember the hikes Father made us take?"

Elsa closes her eyes, nods. "We were so exhausted, and he wouldn't give us water. He would mention his long marches through France and the Balkans; compared to that, our six-hour hikes in the heat of summer were pleasant strolls." Elsa takes a sip from her own wineglass. "His droning about how they marched 2,300 kilometers in the suffocating heat. Our family forest hikes prepared us for deprivation. In his mind, there was always war or war approaching. He was a fierce man."

The pronouncement surprises me. I've never questioned Elsa's devotion to Father; I believed that in her eyes, he could do no wrong.

Elsa walks to a computer in the study; I follow. She scans the internet for more information she has unearthed in her quest for the past.

"Do you remember when Father said that in Russia, the face of the war changed?" Elsa asks, her eyes toward the computer screen. "That that is where the real fighting began?"

"I remember."

"The second medal here . . ." she says and holds up the badge, "was for his achievements during the fight for Crimea."

Crimea. So much had changed since the Second World War. And so little. In 2017, Crimea is still disputed territory between Russia and the Ukraine. The conflict over Crimea is not the only disturbing echo from the past. In Germany, a new right-wing party, the AfD, is gaining traction thirty years after the wall fell. With Hitler's rising, my home country had attracted a sickness and has been only partly successful in healing from its tumultuous, painful past. In my adopted country, Donald Trump was recently elected president. In the lead-up to the Second World War, democracy emptied itself, giving way to charismatic leaders who promised the world and thought only of themselves. So many people haven't seen the signs, and the atmosphere reminds me of the time before Hitler came to power.

Watching these poisonous ideas infect the minds of people around me is a continual source of distress. I think of Michelle when he said about Nazi Germany: "You have to make sure this never happens again." I shiver. At least I have fulfilled my silent promise and gave my first child a Jewish name. I will always defend democracy, one of the only systems where people can live together peacefully and have freedom of speech.

Elsa has pulled up a map of Crimea on the computer.

"After Germany conquered France, Father's division marched for months through the Balkans. They finally reached the Romanian-Russian frontier by train at the end of July 1941. They battled their way to the Crimea peninsula. Elsa peers at the Crimean map more closely. "At the beginning of December when winter started, they'd lost more than half of their men. They were not prepared for the season. Some of them froze to death without warm winter coats. Still, they conquered the town Kerch"— Elsa moves her mouse over the city— "but only for a few weeks. The Russians were larger in number and came out on top. Another four months later, Dad's division got another troop enforcement and they officially conquered Kerch."

"Crimea has strategic value because it's on the Northern Coast of the Black Sea," Elsa continues.

"But it also gives access to the Mediterranean, the Balkans, and the Middle East. It opened the way for Hitler to get to Russia," I add to the conversation.

I take the medal from the desktop and examine it. 1941–1942. Something is not adding up.

"Dad said Hitler cared about family trees. He got sent home from Russia because he was his family's only son, and his father had died in the First World War. But you're saying Father fought in Crimea for almost a year and that he earned a medal for it?"

Elsa turns slowly to me, nods. "I've done the research." She sighs. "I've learned so much about traumatic reenactment—how Father replayed the traumas he experienced in the war, how he passed those traumas on to us, and how we played out the script too. I had to know what really happened. I had to break the cycle, to heal."

I have never heard the term *traumatic reenactment*, but then things click into place for me. The term instantly brings light, new understanding on why I had struggled so bitterly as a new mother—my depression, my rage toward my sons. Perhaps I had been replaying traumas I inherited from Father and Mother too.

I've dealt with my own stable of therapists, read dozens of self-help books. A few years ago, I finally found a life coach: someone who could help me deal with my struggles as a parent. Since beginning with my coach, I've encountered my own power to create *new* patterns. I've experienced so much healing. Still, I've never heard of *traumatic reenactment*.

"My research has helped me understand Dad better. Why he was such a despot," says Elsa.

"And what about Mom? Do you understand her better too? She was only a child during the war times."

Elsa's face darkens. "I hate Mom. Always did. She didn't protect us from him. She was only looking out for herself."

I offer no comment to Elsa's view of Mom, which I don't

share. I bear no bitterness toward Mom, although I don't believe she ever really loved me. She never said the words, and I never felt a bond between us. Yet the last memory I have of Mom a few months before she died is a good one: the evening prior to my family's departure for the States, she and I had dined with the kids at an Italian restaurant with a view of the Halensee lake in Berlin. It was a perfect summer evening. Afterward, Mom drove us back to the hotel where we stayed. "See you next year," she'd said, hugging me with a kind, sad smile. I stood on the sidewalk in front of the hotel with my sons, waving until Mom's car slipped out of sight. Even now, I can see her hand waving back, her smile in the rear mirror.

Mom had difficulties truly loving anyone due to her own difficult childhood. I don't hate her for her lack of love. I simply accept that she was only able to give us the meager amount of care she possessed. At any rate, I leave Mom out of the discussion with Elsa. The talk of Father stirs up enough pain.

"Anyway." Elsa folds her hands across her lap. "I wanted to show you what I've learned."

I glance at Elsa. The years fall away—all at once, I see the young girl who hid under the sink as Father covered her naked back with red welts from his oversized hand. I do not see the hard working doctor, the suburbanite, and Father's favorite who could destroy me with a withering word. I know this is her way of apologizing for all the times she has betrayed me in the past. In this moment, I feel sorry for Elsa and all that she has suffered.

"One winter, Father showed me how to protect my feet from freezing." I close my eyes and there we are, me slipping on my winter boots to hike for god-knows-how-long in the snow. "Father took my feet and wrapped them in newspaper, then slipped them back into the boots. 'There is nothing more bitter than cold,' he said." I open my eyes, catch Elsa's gaze. "I am sure he was thinking of his comrades."

Elsa nods. "There was a fight near Kerch. 13,000 Russians hid in a stone quarry for 170 days. They ran out of food and water. At night, they came to the surface to get water from a well." She swallows. "I think Dad must have been involved in a battle there. The Russians tried to raid the German camp. There was no space for the Germans to take Russian prisoners, so the Germans had to shoot them."

I imagine the scene with Russians coming out of the ground, trying to get water and food, trying to kill their enemies, the Germans. This must have been a nightmare for both sides and my own nightmares of the men in the black uniforms now make so much more sense to me.

"Doctors know how to shoot someone," Elsa continues. "The most efficient way to do it is to shoot them in the neck. It's clean; the person is dead in a second."

I see a new picture of Father, starving Russians kneeling before him as he aims the gun and pulls the trigger with an executioner's precision. I feel the metal of the pistol against my own neck. But I will never know if Elsa's accusations are true.

Another image—Father's flashing blue eyes filling with rage for some childhood indiscretion of mine, perhaps wearing my Carnival dress too early in the morning. Father had looked as if he wanted to kill me. The same fury had moved through me when I had been unable to comfort my toddler son, when I'd been subjected to his wails for hours and hours with no one to help me care for him.

I shudder at the memory of the surging violence inside of me.

"Are you sure this is true?" I ask Elsa.

"Yes, Anne. I've done the research. Dad applied for deployment to Russia. He wanted to be with his comrades."

By then, Father's troop had been together for more than a year. I suppose the thought of being left behind was more terrifying than the thought of dying at the enemy's hand in a brutal Russian winter.

Elsa looks at her lap. "I am also convinced Father knew about the Holocaust." She rubs her forefinger and thumb together. "The Crimea is a small peninsula. During the fighting in 1941, 6,000 Jews had been killed there. I doubt that Father didn't know."

Something settles inside of me. Why wasn't I surprised? My willful naivete as a child had served as protection. I could not accept what Father had done, and so I had reasoned that he couldn't have done it. But I am in my fifties now; I am willing to let my childhood illusions fall away, however painful that may be.

Elsa continues, "He returned to Germany in 1942. He was deployed near Nuremberg and working for the Wehrmacht as a doctor, examining troops for their medical fitness. Then he sent them to war."

I had asked Father so many times about his work after Russia. Only once had he given me a glimpse into his blurry past, when he had told me about transporting the files from Nuremberg to Munich, the bomb that had killed his fellow soldiers. He never said what the files were, yet I had gathered that it was material that needed to be protected from the Allies.

After Father's death, my sisters and I had discovered letters he had written to his mother. From those, we learned that Father had hid from the Allies for at least a year after the war and had moved to Berlin. In his letters, he had avoided mentioning *why* he hid. Perhaps he feared the Allies or the police would open his mail.

"I believe the police were looking for him," Elsa continues. "He was sending doctors into war until Germany surrendered. Sending young men to their deaths. He believed in the war till the bitter end. Families in Nuremberg hated him for that.

Father could have helped young men by taking them out of service, but he didn't."

At long last, the puzzle pieces fit together. There is no way to beautify Father's ugly history, the history we carry. I finally see the past for what it is. I hope that Elsa is right—that her quest for the truth will enable us to heal, to release the strangle hold the past has on us.

The sounds of our children playing ping pong in the basement float up towards us.

"I have made so many mistakes. And I've likely passed on Father's trauma to my children. But if I can heal, perhaps so can they," Elsa says.

I have struggled mightily with intimacy and love all my adult life. Perhaps if Father and Mother could have spoken truthfully about their experiences—about their guilt, grief, and shame—things would be different in our household; I would not now be replaying the traumas I learned under their roof. But as Germans, they were not able to do this. Only recently, over half a century after the war, had older Germans begun to speak publicly about their experiences. Germans were the instigators and losers of two World Wars and were responsible for the Holocaust; they could not grieve publicly. Yet so much pain had been transmitted behind closed doors.

The term *traumatic reenactment* has given me a sense of relief. For so long, I've thought that my mistakes as a mother were all mine. I have been unable to confront my grief. As my father had, I've clenched my teeth and swallowed my emotions. I will need courage to confront the source of my pain, to continue the healing process. Courage and patience.

Patience I have. In my years away from home, I have become a long-distance runner. I know what it is to bear with the feelings of uncertainty and fatigue, to put one foot in front of the other despite how irresistible the allure of stopping. The work of healing is not done in a moment; it is a marathon, at times grueling, but at its finish line is hope. Happiness. Freedom from the past and the promise of living at peace in the present moment.

Darkness has long since fallen outside; it is well after midnight. Tiredness hits me like a wave. I thank Elsa for all that she had shared. I fall asleep to the gentle pitter-patter of the ping pong ball hitting the table.

EPILOGUE

Santa Monica, California

The *buzz buzz* of my cell phone sounds from the kitchen counter. I pick it up and hear a voice I have not heard in six months.

"Anne? This is Tara."

Tara. My former life coaching client, who recognized that she needed therapy before she could move forward with coaching in any meaningful way. It's good to hear her voice, and I tell her so. "How are you?"

Tara breathes deeply. Unlike six months ago, her breaths are slow and steady—not choked with sobs. "I'm much better than I was the last time we talked," she laughs. "Six months ago, it was as if a bomb had gone off in my life."

"Having a baby can feel that way," I say. "No one tells you that. I guess they don't want to scare people off from it!"

Tara and I share a laugh.

"I started seeing a therapist," says Tara, and I nod. Just from her voice, I can tell that Tara has been receiving support. She sounds more upbeat and lighthearted.

"How has that been?"

"I've gone once a week for the past six months. At first, I felt terrible for needing therapy after the baby. I didn't think I would have postpartum depression, so I had all this shame when I realized I *did* have it. And it took me a while to even admit that's what it is."

I choose my words carefully. "And how do you feel about it now?"

"Well, the shame is gone," says Tara. "My therapist helped me to understand how life-altering childbirth can be. That word you used when we spoke six months ago—traumatic. My therapist used it too, which helped me to accept it. Having Daniel caused a traumatic disruption to my world, even though I was so ready to be a mom. And it brought back all these traumas from childhood that I thought I'd moved past."

"It's amazing what a big life disruption can unearth," I say. "It's like a tornado, coming through and rearranging an entire town. Survivors always say that after the tornado, they found strange things in the debris—things they hadn't thought about in decades."

"Yes, that's *exactly* what it was like." Tara releases a big sigh, the relief in her voice evident. "In the early-early days of Daniel's life, I felt an overwhelming need to control. Probably because there's nothing like a baby to make you realize how little control you have." She pauses. "It reminded me of my mom, which scared the hell out of me. She was so desperate to control everything about my sister and me—what we ate, how we dressed, what music we listened to, and where we went after school. Everything. And it's all because she was terrified. She came from nothing, then rose to this upper middle class country club lifestyle, and I think she was terrified people would find out about her past and realize that . . . " Tara laughs. "Can you tell my therapist and I have been talking all about this?"

I laugh too. "It sounds like you've been doing good work!"

"Yes," says Tara, and I can hear the enthusiasm in her voice. "I've been thinking about the future again. In a good way, not a scary way. All the things that were on my mind when I first came to you."

I smile. "Tell me what you're thinking."

Tara begins to talk about her dreams: how she's returned to her job in human resources, but her heart is no longer in it. How since Daniel's birth, she feels she's meant to do so much more; she's thinking about starting her own business. Tara talks about her friendships, how she'd like them to be deeper. Now that she's a mom, she sees the need for more meaningful community and recognizes the ways in which her current community doesn't cut it. Tara feels she's on the precipice of many changes—exciting, longed-for changes—but she doesn't know how she'll get from where she is to where she wants to be. The "hows" scares her; but she believes a more aligned life is possible.

I recognize in her voice the same excitement I felt at the start of my own impossible journey: founding a school. When my sons were in early grade school, I was sorry that there was no German bilingual school in Los Angeles.

Wishing soon gave way to thinking, *What if?* I met other parents in the German community who shared my desire. We learned about a school in San Diego, an international baccalaureate school where students learned German, and teachers took a project-based approach to learning. Students at the San Diego school learned how to be global citizens, driven to learn by their own enthusiasm and curiosity. It sounded like heaven; I wished there were something like that in Los Angeles for Ariel and Tim.

Through discussions with other parents, we realized that the interest was there; For the next two years, I immersed myself in co-founding the school my sons would eventually attend. It was like working an unpaid job while simultaneously receiving a graduate degree in nonprofit management. Each day, I would work for a small business, care for the kids in the afternoon, and then stay up until midnight contacting various persons of interest engaged in the project, reaching out to potential parents from whom I'd drummed up interest or doing research for the school's charter.

The other co-founders and I committed to our shared vision and we held on when egos got bruised, conflicts arose, and endless amounts of red tape threatened to stop our project before it could get off the ground. We built friendships for a lifetime. When the school opened, it wasn't perfect. Yet we were all so thrilled with the accomplishment. I'd gone from wishing my children could have a different education, to creating the environment in which I thought they could best succeed.

Tara today reminds me of where I was back then: on the verge of big, exciting change. She is recognizing her power to create the future she envisions.

"There is so much I want to be and do," says Tara, and I can hear the yearning in her voice, the hope for the future which is just out of frame. "If someone could lay out a step-by-step plan for me, I would do it. No questions asked."

"Wouldn't it be nice if we all had that!" I say.

"Right?" Tara laughs. "I want to be everything. All the ways I've been holding back—I don't want to do that anymore. Not with Daniel in the picture."

"But who you've been up to this moment—it's good," I say. "It's enough. You holding Daniel and feeling happy—that's the best gift you could ever give him. In life coaching, we start with the present moment. We accept it for what it is, with gratitude. From there, we move forward."

Tara inhales, exhales. "I get what you're saying. My anxiety doesn't help anybody."

"Luckily, we can move forward and drop the anxiety. Life

coaching begins with acceptance, of where you are now and where you've been. From there we can move forward."

"I think I can do that," Tara says. "Or at least, I can learn. The therapy is helping so much—I'm finally coming to terms with my past."

I think of my own past: Father's house and the dark spell it cast, how the process of freeing myself began on the day I woke up after swallowing the sleeping pills and decided I had to change. How even with that decision, the work of breaking the cycle of traumatic reenactment, loving myself, and owning my power has taken decades—and it's still unfinished.

"Coming to terms with the past," I repeat. "That's the work of a lifetime."

"Yes," says Tara. "I think I'm getting that. There will always be more to uncover and heal, but that's okay. *I'm* okay. And no matter what my past has looked like before, I get to write my story going forward. I'm the one who decides."

I can't keep the smile from my lips. In my mind's eye, I see all the beautiful things life has in store for Tara—and now she can see them too. There is no more exciting moment than when a person decides to step up to the plate and claim the wonderful future that everyone deserves. This is that moment for Tara; I am honored to be her guide. I have only one final question for her.

"Shall we begin?"

ACKNOWLEDGMENTS

After many years the journey of writing my story comes to an end. It all started on a five days writing retreat with UCLA Extension at Lake Arrowhead and the picture of my father's two medals that I had taken with me from Germany. Since that time I met many wonderful people who greatly supported me in making this book happen.

First, and foremost, I want to express my gratitude to Jennifer Locke. I wouldn't have finished this book without you. I thank you for believing in my original version and your insightful edits that helped give shape to an unshaped mess.

I am also deeply grateful to the coterie of talented editors who helped midwife this book into the world: Kathleen Furin, Shaina Clingempeel and Nika Rose.

I want to thank my distinguished Saturday writer's group for their patient critiques of my many drafts that helped me constantly improving my work: James Garbanati, Alexandra Levine, Lena Nelson, Michelle Peterson, Jean Richardson, Valerie Silverio, Nora Sun and most of all Lauren Tyler who has taken on and facilitating these meetings in the weird time called Covid. You made this group possible. Thank you for sharing with us your knowledge and expertise. I admire your work as a poet.

I also want to thank Barbara Abercrombie for the enlightening writer's workshops at the Vroman's bookstore and at UCLA Extension. Your insightful comments on my work were invaluable to me.

Last but not least, I want to thank Stephanie Larkin, owner of Red Penguin Books, for taking me under her wings and giving me the chance to publish my story.

ABOUT THE AUTHOR

Born in Germany, Anne-Christine Witzgall grew up in West-Berlin and worked in Paris, Munich and Berlin before moving with her husband to Santa Monica over 15 years ago. She is a Board Certified Coach (BCC), a life coach specialist and holds a masters degree in journalism with minors in sociology and psychology. She sees her role as that of a guiding light helping people discover their purpose, act on their dreams and live their best lives. She's been passionately invested in supporting others harness their full potential for over a decade already as a writer, educator and business woman – she's the co-founder of Los Angeles' Goethe International Charter School – work that led her seamless transition into life coaching.

Anne-Christine has two young adult children, and outside of coaching and teaching can be regularly found on the tennis court, writing or reading, and hanging out with her two rescue dogs.

FREEING RAPUNZEL is Anne's first book. Her memoir is about how she escaped the shadows of her family's Nazi past during the cold war era in West Berlin, Germany.

www.ingramcontent.com/pod-product-compliance
Lightning Source LLC
Chambersburg PA
CBHW071235070526
44583CB00017B/2197